Every so often a book comes across our desks that contests what we have accepted to be the thinking and practice of Political Science. This book does precisely that as it sets a courageous tone that challenges as it clarifies. This is what Kassab has done with this important text. As students, practitioners, and academics, we are tasked with making sense of how we got to this point in international affairs. We do not stop there, but rather also set out to both predict and try to shape the coming future. Kassab takes issue with this accepted approach by methodically showing its shortcomings and failures. A must read, this book presents both a challenge to the way we think about the field and a necessary way forward.

Dr. Hasmet Uluorta, *Chair of the Department of Political Studies, Trent University*

Post-Cold War Predictions

Post-Cold War Predictions examines how the international order evolved after the collapse of the Soviet Union (and before the attacks on 9/11) by focusing on the ways we study and understand major powers' security behavior within the evolving multipolar order. Beginning with an overview of Post-Cold War literature, Kassab summarizes and evaluates influential Post-Cold War texts to better understand scholarship's need to predict. First, he discusses the central importance of power in international relations and drives home the central focus of international structures, linking findings to the broader structure-agent problem. He then reinterprets the purpose of theory, preferring explanatory theories to those that aim to predict outcomes. To understand the context by which political ideas were developed and followed as if they were political ideologies, Hanna Samir Kassab makes explicit the links between historicism and historiography, forwarding a new methodology for studying political science: Politicist analysis. Using simple jargon and defining terms where necessary, this succinct and enlightening text is required reading for all those interested in international politics.

Hanna Samir Kassab is Assistant Professor of political science and security studies at East Carolina University, USA.

Routledge Advances in International Relations and Global Politics

Gender Inequality & Women's Citizenship
Evidence from the Caribbean
Yonique Campbell and Tracy-Ann Johnson-Myers

Strategic Culture(s) in Latin America
Explaining Theoretical Puzzles and Policy Continuities
Edited by Félix E. Martín, Nicolás Terradas and Diego Zambrano

Brazilian Agricultural Diplomacy in the 21st Century
A Public-Private Partnership
Niels Søndergaard

Neutral Europe and the Creation of the Nonproliferation Regime
1958–1968
Edited by Pascal Lottaz and Yoko Iwama

Australian Politics at a Crossroads
Prospects for Change
Edited by Matteo Bonotti and Narelle Miragliotta

Post-Cold War Predictions
Politicism in Practice
Hanna Samir Kassab

For information about the series: www.routledge.com/Routledge-Advances-in-International-Relations-and-Global-Politics/book-series/IRGP

Post-Cold War Predictions
Politicism in Practice

Hanna Samir Kassab

Routledge
Taylor & Francis Group
NEW YORK AND LONDON

First published 2024
by Routledge
605 Third Avenue, New York, NY 10158

and by Routledge
4 Park Square, Milton Park, Abingdon, Oxon, OX14 4RN

Routledge is an imprint of the Taylor & Francis Group, an informa business

Library of Congress Cataloging-in-Publication Data
Names: Kassab, Hanna Samir, 1984– author.
Title: Post-Cold War predictions: politicism in practice / Hanna Samir Kassab.
Description: First edition. | New York : Routledge, 2024. |
Series: Routledge advances in international relations and global politics |
Includes bibliographical references and index. |
Summary: "Post-Cold War Predictions examines how the international order evolved after the collapse of the Soviet Union (and before the attacks on 9/11) by focusing on the ways we study and understand major powers' security behavior within the evolving multipolar order. Beginning with an overview of Post-Cold War literature, Kassab summarizes and evaluates influential Post-Cold War texts to better understand scholarship's need to predict. First, he discusses the central importance of power in international relations and drives home the central focus of international structures, linking findings to the broader structure-agent problem. He then reinterprets the purpose of theory, preferring explanatory theories to those that aim to predict outcomes. To understand the context by which political ideas were developed and followed as if they were political ideologies, Hanna Samir Kassab makes explicit the links historicism with historiography, forwarding a new methodology for studying political science: politicist analysis. Using simple jargon and defining terms where necessary, this succinct and enlightening text is required reading for all those interested in international politics"– Provided by publisher.
Identifiers: LCCN 2023051758 (print) | LCCN 2023051759 (ebook) |
ISBN 9781032743158 (pbk) | ISBN 9781032732824 (hbk) |
ISBN 9781003468677 (ebk)
Subjects: LCSH: Multipolarity (International relations) |
Security, International. | Legitimacy of governments. |
Failed states. | Non-state actors (International relations) | World politics.
Classification: LCC JZ1312.2 .K365 2024 (print) |
LCC JZ1312.2 (ebook) | DDC 327–dc23/eng/20231201
LC record available at https://lccn.loc.gov/2023051758
LC ebook record available at https://lccn.loc.gov/2023051759

ISBN: 978-1-032-73282-4 (hbk)
ISBN: 978-1-032-74315-8 (pbk)
ISBN: 978-1-003-46867-7 (ebk)

DOI: 10.4324/ 9781003468677

Typeset in Times New Roman
by Newgen Publishing UK

To Hasmet Uluorta: professor, mentor, and friend.

Contents

1 Introduction

At significant critical junctures in international affairs, scholars, policymakers, and thinkers, in general, seek new ways of understanding world politics. This is especially true in recent history. In *Aftershocks: Pandemic Politics and the End of the Old International Order,* authors Colin Kahl and Thomas Wright submit that the old international system of states was useless in containing the spread of Covid-19. They recommend building global governance mechanisms that enhance future cooperation. After the First World War, many hoped for a new world based on the liberal principles of Woodrow Wilson's *Fourteen Points.* Competition would be replaced with cooperation facilitated by a new international body called the League of Nations.

Similarly, in the mystery of the Post-Cold War era, many began to think of future possibilities. Some scholars predicted the potential of perpetual peace and prosperity; others doom and gloom. There would simultaneously be an "end of history" (Fukuyama, 1992) celebration as well as a "clash of civilizations" (Huntington, 1997). Marxists worldwide saw the beginning of an empire without a center (Hardt & Negri, 2000). Huntington's work, *The Clash of Civilizations"* (1997), begins in a very peculiar way. He argues that a civilization approach may help understand politics in the late twentieth and early twenty-first centuries. Such a note may strike the reader as odd as this book was published in 1996, a mere five years after the collapse of the Soviet Union. However, if one was reading in 1997, isolating civilizational trends occurring before the Soviet Union's collapse might offer a glimpse into the future. However, it is difficult to establish whether or not these trends would last, as contemporary historians are part

DOI: 10.4324/9781003468677-1

of the history they are studying. I would argue that Huntington's approach and effort were premature. Other scholars to be discussed in this book followed Huntington's approach centering mostly on prediction (something that Huntington either set out to do or did so unknowingly). However, he started an interesting conversation many felt obliged to praise and deride. Renowned historian Eric Hobsbawm understands this difficulty as his preface to "Age of Extremes: The Short Twentieth Century 1914–1991) opens:

> Nobody can write the history of the twentieth century like that of any other era, if only because nobody can write about his or her lifetime as one can (and must) write about a period known only from outside, at second or third-hand from sources of the period of the works of later historians.
>
> (Hobsbawm 1995, ix)

It is indeed difficult, but not impossible, as Hobsbawm's work attests. One would assume prediction would be far more difficult given the complexity of understanding contemporary reality.

This book is experimental and forwards a new methodology for studying political science: Politicist analysis. It examines the literature of the Post-Cold War period in depth. Drawing on Karl Popper (1961), historicist arguments see history as connected to the future. Politicist arguments are those that predict the future based on specific interpretations of the current political order and the reigning ideology. Politicist analysis combines historicism with historiography to understand the political context by which political ideas are developed and followed as if they were political ideologies. For instance, the enthusiasm for the new world order after the Cold War led to American economic, ideological, and military expansion bolstered by unipolarity and beliefs of exceptionalism. There was a real hope that American capitalism and democracy would usher in a peaceful, more prosperous world. That very enthusiasm shaped scholarship, informing hypotheses and sculpting data interpretation. Marxist writers may bemoan the fall of the Soviet Union and see unbridled capitalism as a threat to people (Hardt and Negri 2000). Politicist analysis studies the political-cultural context of the time of writing, especially with the benefit of hindsight. It allows for a better understanding of that day's scholarship. Such a methodology requires a deep, close reading of someone's work. Politicism allows scholars the opportunity to re-examine and test the validity of a previous work, identifying both the strengths and weaknesses of such an argument. This book revisits influential Post-Cold War texts and "tests" them to better understand the present. It also examines scholars' need to predict. Predictions about the evolution of the international order after the collapse of the Soviet Union were nullified after the attacks on 9/11.[1] 9/11 is an anomaly that pushed many to focus on non-state threats like terrorism while seemingly ignoring challenges from other states like China and Russia. United States interventions in Afghanistan and Iraq led to its decline, leading to the rise of China and the resurgence of Russia (Shifrinson 2020; Pavlova 2018). What ever happened to the arguments predicting the future of the international order? The End of History? The Clash of Civilizations? Empire? The Unipolar Moment? Evaluating scholar arguments with the Politicist methodology then may help us better understand the current multipolar international system. Hence, this book seeks to connect the post-Cold War era before the attacks on 9/11 to current conversations on world order, specifically discussions on the rise of China, the resurgence of Russia, and the absolute and relative decline of the United States.

The book also isolates the main mechanisms of international politics, which seem to be the structure of anarchy and the need to remain independent and secure through military power. After the collapse of the Soviet Union, it is clear that the United States, a hegemonic state, threatened other great powers, specifically Russia and China (Shifrinson 2020; Pavlova 2018; Mearsheimer 2006). These significant powers strove to balance against the more potent form, reshaping the structure of the international system from unipolarity to multipolarity. Hegemony is thus temporary. States may try to prolong their hegemonic position, but such endeavors may eventually prove fruitless. A hegemonic state may not be able to constrain all the states in the system all the time. Eventually, those most upset with the system will seek to transform or overturn it, even if those states materially benefit from that system.

1 This has long been a passion even during my undergraduate years. Assigned essays would request some analysis of international security, which I would faithfully begin. However, as the essay rolled on, I would revert to discussing competing ideas of twenty-first-century international relations.

Purpose of Book: Politicist Analysis Methodology

Politicist analysis examines the political context by which works of Political Science are shaped and manufactured. Scholars write within a specific political time and context, like all human beings. Sometimes their feelings toward a particular topic will ultimately result in a detailed interpretation of data. This interpretation of data may take on all the traits of the scientific method providing legitimacy. Fukuyama, Friedman, Callinicos, Rice, and Krauthammer all reflect this dynamic. Dedication toward a specific framework or theory shapes scholars' understanding of a particular event. A Marxist may see the world as inherently based on class struggle, so all aspects of life might be perceived in that specific way. The same goes for a liberal who may view free trade and democracy as the answer to all the world's problems; these may even go so far as to support regime change in authoritarian states leading to suboptimal international security outcomes (power vacuums and proliferation of terrorist networks, i.e., Post 2003 Iraq and Islamic State or today's Libya). Indeed, much of the Post-Cold War literature might be summarized by key ideological words such as neoliberal, neoconservative, Marxist, and so on. In many ways, theories of international relations, economics, or any theory of the social sciences are much more than simply mental images, as Waltz purports but act as political ideologies that are borderline religious. These religions or church denominations limit our understanding of the world because they abstract the world, creating simple models. In many respects, scholars who received advanced degrees help bring order and understanding to a very complicated and noisy world. While many writers try to be objective, one cannot escape the fact that human beings are imperfect creatures with a specific nature and normative desire. These might be a product of upbringing; it is a social construction. Some degree of psychological analysis of those writing; the frame of mind of the authors is always of interest. The proposed methodology will not go deeply into that person's history but rather into that person's interpretation of those events. It is not the person that matters but their interpretation of events as a continuity of past performances. Politicist analysis effort is not simply to understand the perspectives but to analyze, critique, and reevaluate the process by which these perspectives are formulated. The process of theorizing is at the center of any scholarship. Before defining Politicist analysis, it is important to first define theories to fully understand the process of misrepresenting the scientific method.

Theories and Theory-Building Defined

Theories are simply a collection of assumptions explaining specific phenomena. There are descriptive or explanatory theories and those that aim to predict. Kenneth Waltz submits three rudimentary propositions of explanatory theories:

1 A theory contains at least one theoretical assumption (which might not be true, only applicable).
2 Theories must be evaluated in terms of what they claim to explain.
3 Theories cannot account for particularities (Waltz 2010, 119).

Waltz defines theory as "a picture, mentally formed, of a bounded realm or domain of activity. A theory is a depiction of the organization of a domain and the connection of its parts" (Waltz 2010, 8). An assumption is not a statement of fact but one that facilitates explanation through simplification. Every theory makes assumptions about the world to come to some expected conclusions about the world. Realism believes that states are motivated by security concerns, while liberals give more weight to economic prosperity. Marxists assume that class struggle is at the center of all politics. Social constructivists accept that social interactions form the basis of political outcomes. Gendered approaches make their assumptions about the importance of women's voices. Post-structuralists may not admit that they generalize, but by refusing to generalize, they are still taking on an assumption: generalizations are dangerous. Here, we see the importance of making assumptions.

Theorizing is at the center of social science and the human experience. It is natural to make assumptions about the world. In our everyday lives, we make certain assumptions about the world. We can disagree about the assumptions made by other people and make our own. For instance, as Organski notes, states are not unitary actors, as Waltz assumes. This is obvious as states are sometimes split across ethnic, class, party, ideological, linguistic, and other lines. However, erasing that assumption eliminates the attempt at explanation, and we return to the starting position. Given this, new theories emerge, and old ones die, replaced by better ones in Kuhnian fashion. However, this does not mean that all theories should be accepted; theory testing is as necessary as theory building. A theory must be successfully applied to some cases to be considered relevant. Further, theories must be falsifiable; no theory can explain every and all event. Realism works well to present interstate conflicts, such as the Ukraine conflict. It will have difficulty explaining cooperation and the formulation for the European Union, for example. Liberalism may be better suited to examine why certain states cooperate while others do not.

Some theories aim to predict. Prediction is not entirely a fool's errand. Of course, in retrospect, one may believe so, especially given some of the works studied in this book. Prediction is different from historicist or politicist works. Reliable predictions account for various possibilities backed by evidence, assumptions, and parameters. In Martin Hollis' *The Philosophy of Science,* he distinguishes between explanatory and predictive theories. Milton Friedman's monetary economics theory is a prime example of a predictive theory. As said, Waltz's Structural Realism is an example of explanatory theory. Each theory has specific aims even with the overlap. Waltz hoped to explain state survival behavior, including internal and external balancing, culminating in a balance of power. It explains why states balance against one another. It is incorrect to say that Structural Realism failed to predict the end of the Soviet Union. A theory cannot do everything like predict state collapse; that is not what Waltz set out to do. Structural Realism does fail to account for international political change, but other theories forwarded by Gilpin and Organski do. Friedman's economic theory aimed to predict inflation given increases in the money supply. Friedman's work targets the central importance of money in the political economy, given the experiences in the 1970s and 1980s. Friedman gained incredible popularity for his message and transformed our understanding of the macroeconomy, even though international governing organizations and regimes largely ignore his notice.

Prediction must account for multiple outcomes; one thing does not necessarily lead to one single eventuality, but rather several potential consequences are given intervening variables. An increase in the money supply may not result in inflation if people are willing to hold that currency worldwide, reflected in increased demand. A decrease in the money supply may not result in deflation or unemployment if people decide not to have that currency. Prediction must be done with humility and not with complete certainty, as historicist or politicist writers tend to do. While explanatory and predictive theories may want to influence policy-makers, as we all tend to do, it is done with some respect for the scientific method. Further, confusion about theory has led to people thinking that theories are useless or not practical. Theories instead give some much-needed order to the world. Theories do not equate to truth or reality but are simplified reflections or images of that reality. It is a shadow or an abstraction. War with China is not inevitable, but works forwarded by persons like Graham Allison's Thucydides Trap may try to convince us of just such an inevitability (Allison 2015). Allison believes that

> Based on the current trajectory, a war between the United States and China in the decades ahead is not just possible but much more likely than recognized at the moment. Indeed, judging by the historical record, war is more likely than not…A risk associated with Thucydides Trap is that business as usual – not just an expected, extraordinary event – can trigger large-scale conflict.
>
> (Allison 2015)

Here, Allison believes that war between the United States and China is more likely than not, given the concept of the *Thucydides Trap*. This sort of determinism is dangerous and represents a false equivalency that might lead to people thinking theoretical prediction equates to the truth. Further, Richard Hanania states that Allison's argument suffers from "unclear definitions, omitted variable bias, and selection bias" (Hanania 2022, 16), making it more pseudoscience than actual social science.

Returning to the role of theory, explanatory theories, and predictive theories must have limitations and be falsifiable. Approaches must clearly outline what they seek to explain, and predictions must have several eventualities, given that the world and its disciplines are complex. Realism is an abstraction of reality, but it is not reality. It is based on assumptions that are neither true nor real but merely helpful, used to explain an event or the relationship between events. However, it must be noted that realism seems to have better marketing power as people, especially students, tend to conflate it for being "real" or "realistic." Realism is certainly not that, as anyone can see that states are not unitary actors. However, it gets close to explaining why states find themselves at war. Liberalism explains cooperation, yet it remains hopeful for change and a new world. It tries to *predict* peaceful outcomes under specific conditions. In this respect, it is much less a theory and has an ideological or normative commitment. This normative commitment may prove dangerous, as demonstrated in Chapter 4.

To summarize, a theory is simply a set of assumptions that try to explain phenomena. There has been a general malaise in international relations since the development of social constructivism. There has been nothing new since then: there has been an application of those theories. There has also been this drive to quantify international politics, especially international political economy. Still, the field has some helpful theories that hope to explain and understand the world. Positivist theories include realism, liberalism, Marxism, and thin constructivism. Post-positivist theories include thicker versions of constructivism (post-structuralism), various gendered perspectives, and post-modernism. All serve as excellent teaching tools in the classroom. Teaching tools are meant to make sense of the events going on in our world. Whatever the theory, there is this effort to simplify our very complex world. Simplification is key to explaining and understanding the world around us.

Politicist Analysis Defined

Politicist analysis combines historicism and historiography to critique scholarship predicting political futures, specifically projections founded on contemporary political structures and the reigning ideology. First, historicism bases the interpretation of facts, events, or any facet of the physical world as deterministic or all part of a broader, possibly inevitable future. In The Poverty of Historicism, Popper explains that historicism is a political effort to shape the future through an interpretation of the past. For instance, when Fukuyama argues for an *end to history*, he is saying that the current state of world order determines the future. He is projecting a specific vision of the future, given the past. In many ways, rational arguments are historicist. For historicists, history is not merely "the presentation of the course of past events…a statement of facts and their effects" (von Mises 1985, 211) but will, not may, direct the course of future events.

Politicist analysis combines historicism with historiography. Historiography studies how historians seek to understand history and the techniques used by a historian: "it is not so much about what happened, but more about how a historical event has been written about, and how that changes depending on who is doing the writing" (Lowery 2016, viii). It is the history of history if you will. It aims to uncover the ways employed by historians that led them to write their historical work. Historiography is a deep study of the results of history itself. Adding the historicist element, politicism seeks to appreciate the frameworks used by authors at a particular historical juncture with the benefit of hindsight. The issue is not simply that authors are biased or leaning toward a specific political outcome but rather a fundamental misunderstanding of theory and theory building in the social sciences.

In his historicist effort, Popper saw historicism as an essential part of authoritarianism, specifically Fascism and Socialism. Robert Nola (1978) sees this as part of Popper's "war effort" against political extremism (1978, 128). More importantly, Popper views historicism as pushing a specific interpretation of the future. He is particularly disturbed by its presence in social sciences, as this discipline helps shape the political future (Popper 1961, 16). Historicism is a specific interpretation of an event as part of a broader future. These perceptions may lead to policies that aim to bring that future into being then. This fatalism may result in destructive policies. In the cases of Fukuyama, Friedman, Rice, and Krauthammer, the 2003 invasion of Iraq could very well have been a product of their arguments that a democratic future is indeed possible, even if it came at the expense of lives. Democracy has to be expanded to protect the liberal democratic future, maintaining order within the specific vision of the writers.

Nola condenses Popper's expectation of historicism's failure, which might then also be extrapolated to this book's contribution of Politicism:

i   There are not any historicist laws based on which such predictions can be made;
ii even if there were, historicists never specify the antecedent conditions which must hold for genuine prediction rather than prophecy;
iii social systems are not sufficiently isolated from influences that upset their normal behavior (Nola 1978, 128).

In the case of Politicism, it might be argued that any attempt at reshaping the world to meet a particular political-ideological view may fail because

i   There are no actual politicist laws based on which such predictions can be made.

While the authors studied in this book are successful, their predictions were ultimately incorrect. They all presumed that the world would be a very different place than it is today. For Friedman and Fukuyama, Russia, China, and Iran would all be democracies. For Huntington, there would be civilizational clashes between the West and the rest. We have instead seen increasing relations between Israel and Gulf Arab states as they attempt to balance against an expansionary Iran. There have also been growing ties between China and Europe, albeit rocky. There was no accurate premise or starting point for each of these arguments. Instead, they were focused more on possible trends given what they perceived as essential variables within their contemporary world order. For Rice and Krauthammer, the emphasis on limiting the proliferation of weapons of mass destruction resulted in the removal of Saddam Hussein in the 2003 Iraq War. Neoconservative ideas entered the White House and Bush's foreign policy doctrine. However, there was very little evidence pointing to Iraq housing these weapons. Together, these three perspectives suffer from faulty premises that lead to diverging opinions about the future of the international order. Marxist scholars identified the class system as the reason for global exploitation, so there is a clear, established historical and empirical divide describing their predictions. These scholars remain Politicist because of their drive to reshape the world order through scholarship, but at least some "science" is behind their suppositions.

The politicist neoliberal, neoconservative, civilizational and Marxist perspectives held assumptions about the world that led to specific predictions of the international order. This leads to the second principle:

ii   Politicists never specify the antecedent conditions for genuine prediction rather than prophecy.

Politicist perspectives described in the book make grandiose assumptions about the world. Instead, they cherry-pick specific cases or instances and then extend those trends to the broader world. Expectations are conceived solely on potential given some trends. In 2008, many thought capitalism was over due to the financial crisis. In a working paper titled *The Global Financial Crisis and a New*

Capitalism? Luiz Carlos Bresser-Pereira argues, "A new democratic capitalist system will emerge, though its character is difficult to predict. It will not be financialized, but the glory years' tendencies toward global and knowledge-based capitalism in which professionals have more say than rentier capitalists, as well as the tendency to improve democracy by making it more social and participative, will be resumed" (2010). Essentially, we have another example of a prediction with no real justification or robust understanding of the political-economic environment. Conversely, some Marxists believe that since capitalism is always in crisis, vested interests will do whatever it takes to strengthen and bolster its support (Hardt and Negri 2000). In Nola's summary of Popper, the term "antecedent conditions" means that there must be some supporting foundations for a prediction actually to take place. Other possibilities or counter-predictions were not made. The works described are fatalist and deterministic, not considering alternatives. Popper sees this as more prophecy rather than social science (Popper 1961, 16). These scholars do not provide any counterargument or explore any other possible vision except their particular vision of society. Given other factors, there is no explanation of the conditions that give rise to their vision of the future or any alternatives that may also occur.

For the works in question, there seems to be some circular logic based on the faults identified by Popper as a historicist. Post-Cold War predictions failed for this reason. Will it be sunny tomorrow because it is sunny today? Weather systems are different from the weather of that day. In the case Post-Cold War scholars:

iii Social systems are not sufficiently isolated from influences that upset their normal behavior (Nola 1978, 128).

Point three summarizes the previous two points and the lack of scholarly rigor. Authors simply take the trends as these conditions meaning they draw on a dependent variable (civilizational conflicts, the proliferation of democracy, end-of-state strife, etc.) to reinforce their dependent variable. Essentially then, there are no robust independent variables being discussed. Thus, the "end of history" hypothesis is true because of the "end of history." Huntington's work suffers from the same issue: there are civilizational conflicts so that the world will be divided into civilizational blocs. Hardt, Negri, and Callinicos make class struggle the center of their analysis. However, their analytical categories are firmly established with years of Marxist scholarship. Neoconservative scholars are probably the worst offenders, making not so much a scholarly argument but an unapologetically American power-based argument for dominating the world's political system for decades. The Neoconservative logic is fundamentally Politicist, formulating violent normative strategies supposedly serving American interests. These arguments adopt the scientific method to enhance legitimacy. When these ideas are put to the test like in Iraq (2003), the result is a remarkable failure.

Politicist analysis revisits past works, summarizing its rationality and testing its validity in the present. It is often worthwhile to do this to understand the nature of scholarship and the process by which scholars seek truth. The following section explores the functioning of this methodology highlighting the need to change the world.

Politicist Analysis: How It Works

Politicism highlights pseudoscience in scholarship focusing on normative structures informing research. Politicist analysis is the historical and ideological analysis of political thought. It shows the relationship between the scholar and scholarship by reading between the lines, revealing not just biases but dedication to a specific framework, shutting out reality in favor of a narrow and simplistic world vision. Many of the works examined in this book are hardly scholarly, even as they take on a form of scholarship. There is a thesis, oftentimes a literature review, and thesis testing with evidence. However, the political/ideological motivation for this research is clear. Making it into *Foreign Affairs* or having a book published may mask the intention of the work to gain the government's ear to change the course of human history. This is what Antonio Gramsci calls praxis. When writing works toward a political goal, Praxis is the aim of historicism and politicism. Voltaire's writing worked hard to influence people's minds toward the French Revolution. Similarly, neoconservative, neoliberal, and Marxist thinkers are working toward that goal. The first two, neoconservative and liberal, work toward an American-dominated century. Marxist thinkers are trying to make a convincing case for academics and other readers to help formulate radical economic and political change. Civilizational scholars are hoping to prepare the world for a divided world, and alliances will be developed based on commonalities and differences defining the possibilities of conflict or cooperation. There is an essentially obvious praxis motivation for politicist arguments: these scholars want to see changes in the world. These changes should reflect their political orientation, creating a world order that closely aligns with their vision. Historicism and Politicism have the same goal: to influence the course of human history.

Gramsci once wrote that "the philosophy of praxis is the absolute historicism…is it along this line that one must trace the thread of the new contemporary world" (Gramsci 1971, 465). Gramsci was actively using his interpretive historical writing to change the world; so too did the authors discussed in this book. This book records the historical and ideological analysis of political thought in many respects. In retrospect, it is clear that many, whether optimistic or pessimistic, tried to uncover the nature of the future. The Cold War was a bloody period, and the hope was that its end would bring new opportunities and challenges. However, rather than discussing the world as is, many decided to try to influence the world with their normative leanings. This proved rather destructive as neoliberal and neoconservative interpretations made their way into American foreign policy. Neoliberal economics led to China's rise and Russia's resurgence through trading networks. At the same time, western misadventures in Iraq, Afghanistan, Libya, Somalia, and other states created failed states and terrorist networks. These pseudo-intellectual exercises aim toward praxis, implementing policies based on political biases for political purposes. Essentially, we got the opposite of what advocates expected: a more dangerous, multipolar world.

In summary, the Politicist methodology critiques scholars' work as having a specific normative-political bias. The term 'politicism' highlights the political-ideological motivation of scholarship. Taking on the cloak of scholarship and using terms such as 'thesis,' 'theory,' or 'framework' adds credibility to their predictions. Like historicism described by Karl Popper, Politicism uncovers does not adopt an array of possibilities but one almost inescapable path. Like historicism, the aim of politicism is praxis. Praxis is about influencing policies to change the world. The *End of History* is more about enforcing a specific vision of the world rather than analyzing the world as it is. As a critique, Politicism holds scholars accountable where appropriate and could be the core of any academic effort.

Chapter Outline

This introductory chapter sets out the aim of this book as an analytical project that teases out the meaning of prediction in theory building within a specific historical moment: the end of the Cold War and the United States' unipolar moment (Krauthammer 1990). It explains that the work presented in chapter 3 is primarily an exercise in what Popper called historicism. Chapter 2 discusses the historical lead-up to the end of the Cold War. It sets the context for the following chapters from a rather pessimistic perspective. Historian Eric Hobsbawm summarizes similar trends that remain constant from the nineteenth through the twentieth century. As a Marxist historian, Hobsbawm appreciates the central position of the global economy, a subject that will come to dominate scholars' attention in the age of globalization. He also focuses a great deal on warfare and perceives that the twenty-first century could be similar. Essentially, he sets the international political and economic terrain to base the theorizing of international politics. To understand today's political environment, we must first understand the evolution of the international system. Chapter 2 prepares us for the subsequent chapters as it identifies important variables like power and state interests. By transposing and critiquing Hobsbawm, we might better understand international systems as they evolve the nature of international political and economic outcomes as is, not as we hope them to be.

Chapter 3 provides a literature review of what I characterize as pessimistic and optimistic scholarship. There is a clear divide between academics seeing the ramifications of the collapse of the Soviet Union and its dominance. For pessimists, the collapse of the Soviet Union will bring complete American power to the world order. This means the United States would act unchecked as there is no counterforce to balance against it. This would result in the unbridled explosion of the free-market economy that would remain in place with little opposition. Others saw the inevitable dominance of American culture, which could bring a civilizational clash between the West and the rest. Others still saw the eventual end of American unipolarity as other states would eventually rise in opposition against it. For optimists, the victory of the United States now meant that democracy and free trade would reign supreme over all other ideologies. These scholars and thinkers are convinced that, given this particular period, the United States could build a superstructure that could safeguard the future of

the human species for years to come. This builds on "American exceptionalism" ideas that posit the United States as a force for good in
the world. As it defends its interests, the United States would act to
protect the interests of all other states and nations in the international
system. These two approaches are flawed because they tried to predict
the future based on their normative underpinnings even as they adopt
the scientific method. The literature chosen in this chapter serves to
illustrate Politicist methodology.

To understand Politicism, we must have the benefit of hindsight.
Chapter 4 evaluates competing perspectives discussed in chapter 4
by summarizing what happened: that the end of history hypothesis
is simply a manifestation of American unipolarity. Power-constructed
globalization and the imperial overstretch of the United States have
led to its unraveling. In this period, the world saw a shift from unipolarity to multipolarity, as the American order proved challenging to
manage in the face of China's rising power and Russia's resurgence.
The structure of the international system's evolution is thus predicated
on the distribution of power across units, and that power shifted away
from the United States to other poles. The structural realist mental picture remains the most powerful explanatory theory, which may have
led to a more correct prediction than others. This chapter will also
explore domestic politics, specifically the rise of Donald Trump and
the incorporation of left-wing ideologies by significant corporations.

Chapter 5 explores the unknown future by describing five
scenarios: whether states will integrate into super-states or disintegrate into smaller states, whether states will continue to compete
under a self-help system or surrender (willingly or unwillingly) to a
one-world government, and whether competing great imperial powers
would create dependencies out of weak states with overlapping loyalties. The final approach offers a concept, *neoempire,* a great power-led
world system that aims to balance against similar units. Such competition for weak states in this manner creates what Hedley Bull referred
to as neo-medievalism. All scenarios are ultimately based on international trends, and none is selected as valid, only possible.

The conclusions consider the intellectual development and diverse
opinions on the possible future over this period. In many ways, no one
scholar was utterly wrong and entirely correct. However, the purpose
of this book is not simply to determine those scholars with a crystal
ball but rather to show that theories are not primarily made for prediction but rather as an explanation. By providing a historical analysis

of political thought in this period, we might be able to understand the world better today. First, we must place aside the predictive aspects of these works and focus only on defining elements. The second part of the conclusions describes the power of theory and theory-building when aimed at explanation. Kenneth Waltz's Structural Realism and views on theory-building are possibly the most appropriate way of creating an approach.

Conclusions and Goals of the Book

This book hopes to evaluate past work to understand international relations' aim fully. As scholars, as Carr (2001) encouraged, we must divide our interpretation of politics between that which is and that which we want to be. Through Politicist analysis we can carefully scrutinize the work of others as they wrote within a specific period. By doing so, we can come up with a better understanding of our increasingly economically integrated yet politically divided world.

This book's main contribution, Politicist Analysis contextualizes today's international system by providing an overview of Post-Cold War literature. It will also highlight the developments of the past thirty years to test said literature to evaluate predictions and expectations. As such, this book has several goals. The first of such plans is to highlight the central importance of power in international relations. Power is defined loosely, adopting Morgenthau's (1985) own understanding of man's control over man. This is essential as Waltz (2010) advocates that power cannot simply be defined as a laundry list. Passion can take many forms, such as economic and reputation (soft), or might take on other conditions, such as dependency (political, economic, cultural, or otherwise). It might be practiced or demonstrated through cyber-realm or blackmail. The main idea is that power is political in that it drives specific outcomes that serve the interests of some at the expense of others.

To highlight the importance of power, this book drives home the central focus of international structures. The international system is still defined by anarchy and security-seeking behavior. All aspects of the global system, whether it be norms that encourage specific behaviors and prohibit others, interdependent economies, or other deep, intrinsic relationships, are subject to power distribution. If states decide to unravel the system due to competing interests, then this is what we shall see. If the system does not change, we cannot expect a new international order predicated on principles of democracy and peace. To expect an "End of History" or "Clash of Civilizations" hypothesis to be accurate, we must first change the international system from anarchy to hierarchy or some other structure. Indeed, anarchy is an assumption of Structural Realism that may or not be valid (only helpful); we must admit that there is no international law or government with an enforcement mechanism other than the power of states. Existing institutions cannot provide justice or stability, which may result in interstate or intrastate wars (for instance, civil wars, which may be part of a broader interstate rivalry). Admitting that anarchy is closer to a fact than a theoretical assumption may help academia realize that there is international political outcomes are not free of military concerns. State interests in terms of power and security still matter. It also cannot be assumed that war is impossible because of economic interdependence. War is a possibility based on states' judgment regarding their political and security goals. War is ultimately politics by other means (Clausewitz, 1984).

Another goal of this book is to conceptualize power within a political context (structure-agent problem). According to Hollis (1994), political change might occur via a foundational structure or by action from actors that created said structure (5). In many respects, it asks where power is located. Since power in its sociological aspects is about control, then *power* must be the ability of a structure to make actors behave in specific ways. Conversely, it might also be the actors' power to shape the structure. The structure has the power to make states behave in particular ways. This means that without the system changing, conflict remains possible. Simultaneously, if actors have the power to change the structure, what prevents them from doing so? If states could change the system, they would have already done so after each significant conflict avoiding the next: World War I, World War II, and the Cold War. In many respects, this book argues that it is possible that Post-Cold War scholars thought that through unipolarity, the system would change altogether. It could also be assumed that globalization would form the new international system. The free movement of goods, capital, people, and their cultures would reshape the world through technologies and free trade international regimes and networks. However, the global system remains in place. This book will thus link the findings of this book to the broader structure-agent problem. This contribution will be expanded further in the conclusions chapter, but it is worth a summary.

This book would also like to focus on the theoretical side of international political thought. In many ways, the scholarship of the Post-Cold War was dominated by prediction. This book would like to reinterpret the purpose of theory, preferring explanatory theories to those that aim to predict outcomes. Explanatory theories aim to "explain" why things happen. This means that explanatory ideas work backward: first, looking at what happened and then coming up with a hypothesis to explain why it happened in the first place. I believe that this is the best we can do as scholars. Prediction is altogether faulty as it uses variables to determine future outcomes. While one may get things right from time to time, to base policy decisions on what the future might be is irresponsible. In many respects, free trade with China may have seemed like an overall linear evolution: China would eventually become more democratic and open due to the benefits of free trade. It was President Bill Clinton who said in a speech justifying China's entry into the World Trade Organization (WTO):

> Bringing China into the WTO and normalizing trade will strengthen those who fight for the environment, labor standards, human rights, and the rule of law.
>
> For China, this agreement will increase the benefits of cooperation and the costs of confrontation.
>
> America, of course, will continue to defend our interests. Still, at this stage in China's development, we will have a more positive influence with an outstretched hand than a clenched fist... Though China may change, we all know it remains a one-party state that denies people the right to free speech and religious expression. We know that trade alone will not bring freedom to China or peace to the world.
>
> That is why permanent normal trade relations must also signal our commitment to permanent change. America will keep pressing to protect our security and advance our values. The vote today is a significant boost to both efforts, for the more China liberalizes its economy, the more it will liberate the potential of its people to work without restraint and to live without fear.
>
> (Clinton 2000, *Associated Press*)

The opposite has happened, and China is increasingly authoritarian domestically and aggressive internationally. Many Post-Cold War visions of the future were canceled by the attacks on 9/11 and the 2008 financial crisis. In many ways, we are back to a multipolar world order similar to the pre-World War I era. Now, who could have predicted that?

The final goal is to illustrate the evolution of the international order, providing context to today's global political environment. It hopes to explain and evaluate past arguments to help understand today's political context. Such work requires a close reading of the scholarship of the time. This is a work of historicism and historiography. It tries to understand the methods scholars use to arrive at their conclusions about the world's future. This methodology hopes to make sense of the historical evolution of the international order as described by the political predictions of the time's academics and thinkers.

References

Allison, G. (2015). "The Thucydides Trap: Are the US and China Headed for War?" *The Atlantic,* September.

Altman, R. (2009). Globalization in Retreat: Further Geopolitical Consequences of the Financial Crisis. *Foreign Affairs Online* <http://www.foreignaffairs.com/articles/65153/roger-c-altman/globalization-in-retreat>

Carr, E.H., (2001). *The Twenty Years Crisis, 1919–1939*, Perennial, New York.

Cerny, P., (1994). "The dynamics of financial globalization: Technology, market structure, and policy response" *Policy Sciences,* 27, 4, 319–342

Clausewitz, C. (1984) On War, eds Michael Howard, Peter Paret, and Bernard Brodie. Princeton University Press, Princeton

Clinton, B., (2000). "President Clinton's Remarks on the Passage of the China Trade Bill" *The Associated Press,* May 25 < https://archive.nytimes.com/www.nytimes.com/library/world/asia/052500clinton-trade-text.html>

Dollar, D. and Kraay, A., (2004). "Trade, Growth, and Poverty" *The Economic Journal,* 114: F22–F49.

Frankel, J., (2000). *Globalization of the Economy* (August). NBER Working Paper No. w7858.

Friedman, T., (1999). *The Lexus and the olive tree.* Farrar, Straus, Giroux, New York

Fukuyama, F. (1992). *The end of history and the last man.* Free Press.

Giddens, A. (2003). *Runaway world: How globalisation is reshaping our lives.* London: Profile.

Gilpin, R., (2001). *Global Political Economy: Understanding the International Economic Order,* Princeton University Press, Princeton

Gramsci A (1971) *Selections from the Prison Notebooks,* Lawrence and Wishart, London.

Hanania, R (2021). "Graham Allison and the Thucydides trap myth" *Strategic Studies Quarterly 15(4)*, 13–24

Hardt, M. & Negri, A. (2000). *Empire*, Harvard University Press, Cambridge

Hardt, M. & Negri, A. (2000). *Empire*, Harvard University Press, Cambridge

Held, D, A, McGrew, Goldblatt, D and J. Perraton., (1999). *Global Transformations: Politics, Economics and Culture*, Stanford University Press, Stanford

Hobsbawm, E. (1995). *Age of extremes: The short twentieth century 1914–1991*, Abacus, London

Hollis, M. (1994). *The philosophy of social science: An introduction*, Cambridge University Press, Cambridge.

Huntingon, S. (1997). *The clash of civilizations and the remaking of the world order*, Simon and Schuster, London.

Huntingon, S. (1997). *The clash of civilizations and the remaking of the world order*, Simon and Schuster, London.

Kennedy, P. M., (1987). *The rise and fall of the great powers: Economic change and military conflict from 1500 to 2000* (1st ed.). Random House.

Keohane, R., & Martin, L., (1995). "The Promise of Institutionalist Theory" *International Security*, 20,1, 39–51

Kindleberger, C., (1973). *The World in Depression, 1929–1939*. Berkeley: University of California Press

Krauthammer, C. (1990). The Unipolar Moment. *Foreign Affairs*, 70(1), 23–33.

Kuhn, T. (1996). *The Structure of Scientific Revolutions*, University of Chicago Press, Chicago.

Lowery, Z. (2016) Historiography (1st ed.). Britannica Educational Publishing, in association with Rosen Educational Services.

McGrew, A & Held, D., (2002). *Governing Globalization: Power, Authority and Global Governance*, Wiley, Hoboken

Mearsheimer, J. J. (2006). 'China's unpeaceful rise', *Current History*, no. 690, 160–162.

Mearsheimer, J. J. (2002). Realism, the Real World, and the Academy. In M. Brecher & F. P. Harvey (Eds.), *Realism and Institutionalism in International Studies* (pp. 23–33). University of Michigan Press.

von Mises, L. (1985). *Theory and history: An interpretation of social and economic evolution*, Ludwig von Mises Institute, Washington DC.

Morgenthau, H. (1985). *Politics Among Nations: The Struggle for Power and Peace*, 6th ed, McGraw-Hill, New York

Morgenthau, H. (1985). *Politics Among Nations: The Struggle for Power and Peace*, 6th ed, McGraw-Hill, New York

Nye, J., (2004). *Soft Power: The Means to Success in World Politics*. Cambridge: Perseus Books Group.

Pavlova, E. (2018). A Russian challenge to multipolarity?: The prospects for political cooperation between Russia and Latin America. Problems of Post-Communism, 65(6), 394–408.

Nola, R (1978). "Popper on historicism and Marxism" *New Zealand Journal of History 12*(2), 124–145.

Popper, K. R. (1961). *The poverty of historicism*. London: Routledge & Kegan Paul.

Shifrinson, J., (2020). "The Rise of China, Balance of Power Theory and US National Security: Reasons for Optimism?" *Journal of Strategic Studies* 43 (2): 175–216.

Waltz, K. (2010). Theory of International Politics, Addison-Wesley Pub. Co, Reading, Mass.

2 The Evolution of the International System

From the Nineteenth to the Twentieth Century

Eric Hobsbawm remains a giant in political history; his *Age of Extremes* is a stunning addition to his "Age of" series, with *Age of Revolution*, *Age of Capital*, and *Age of Empires* as excellent historical summaries of past centuries. *Age of Extremes* is extraordinary as it is about a period he witnessed firsthand. As a historian, Hobsbawm might have given some thought to theorizing. This chapter hopes to theorize on his findings. It will focus on the *Age of Extremes* with particular focus on Part 1, which he describes as the "Age of Catastrophe" and the closing chapter "Towards the Millennium." By applying theory to history, this chapter hopes to trace the evolution of the international system from the nineteenth century to the end of the Cold War to better understand the state dynamics that govern today's global politics. This sets the context for the following chapter by asking the following: given the long and bloody history of the world, how can the international system be changed as forwarded by Fukuyama, Friedman, and so on. As a historian, Hobsbawm might be able to tell us what happened, but he might not be able to tell us why it happened. This chapter describes the *laws* uncovered by Hobsbawm but shows the evolution of the international political order. To reiterate, theories are not the truth but explanations of the truth or why something happened the way it did.

To understand the potential for conflict today, we must first understand the evolution of the international system since the nineteenth century. The underlying thesis for this chapter is that the international system remains a state-centric system that fuses politics and economics to increase control over the rules of the international order. Starting in the nineteenth century, the Concert of Europe hoped to maintain a balance of power by reigning in some of the worst parts

DOI: 10.4324/9781003468677-2

of state competition: war. Its balance of power was designed so that no one control would dominate. After World War I, in the second decade of the twentieth century, the Concert of Europe was replaced by the hegemonic domination of Britain and France at the expense of Germany. Following this, the international system became a bipolar competition between the United States and the Soviet Union. The outcome of this competition was the collapse of the Soviet Union and the rise of the so-called American Century. However, this was not to last, as now we see the beginnings of a multipolar international order.

A close reading of Eric Hobsbawm's *Age of Extremes* (1994) must be conducted to understand the evolving international system. By discussing the tumultuous twentieth century, this chapter sets the context for politicist works discussed in Chapter 3. For example, the hope for a new world after the collapse of the Soviet Union placed too much emphasis on the power of American democracy and capitalism and ignored other possibilities. By isolating the trends and changes discussed by Hobsbawm, we might be better prepared to understand the international political circumstances of today as is, not as we hope they will be. For example, if war is simply politics by other means (Clausewitz 1984), and politics is a question of who gets what (Lasswell 1936), then international politics will be defined by a struggle for power and interests. Any hegemonic international system can be destroyed if it limits revisionist, power-hungry states from attaining their political goals (Gilpin 1988). Similarly, status quo states may choose war if they want to deny revisionist powers from achieving their goals (ibid). Thus, this chapter defines political expectations of the twenty-first century providing a framework to analyze Politicist Post-Cold War literature.

The International System from the Nineteenth to Twentieth Centuries

Before beginning the book, I needed to read the "Bird's Eye View" segment. It consists of epigraph quotes from twelve famous British and European academics, including Isaiah Berlin and William Golding. What stands out is the depressing outlook. Berlin writes, "I have lived through most of the twentieth century without, I must add, suffering personal hardship. I remember it as the most terrible century of Western history" (quoted in Hobsbawm 1994, 1). The quote by Golding follows: "I cannot help thinking that this has been the most violent century in human history" (ibid). In many respects, the twentieth century was a great power conflict, with wars dominating much of the world, from World Wars I and II to the Cold War. The first two wars were destructive to the great powers, as the Cold War was for the rest of the world, specifically the global south.

Interestingly, there is one quote that stands out, one from Nobel Laureate for Science Rita Levi Montalcini: "Despite everything, there have been revolutions for the better in this century, the rise of the fourth estate, and the emergence of women after centuries of repression" (ibid 1). This particular quote stands out as optimistic, contrasting with the others.

Hobsbawm found these particular quotes fascinating, mainly since he notes that a person living in 1990 was better nourished, taller, lived longer, wealthier, healthier, and better educated than their parents, and even more so in 1914 before World War I (ibid 12). In response to his colleagues' quotes, Hobsbawm writes,

> Why then, did the century end, not with a celebration of this remarkable and marvelous progress, but in a mood of uneasiness? As the epigraphs to this chapter show, why did so many reflective minds look back upon it [the twentieth century] without satisfaction, and certainly without confidence in the future?

Hobsbawm responded that it was an extremely violent century especially compared to the nineteenth century.

From Hobsbawm's view, the nineteenth century was a more peaceful one, "a period of almost unbroken material, intellectual, and moral progress ... that has, since 1914, been a marked regression from the standards then regarded as normal ..." (ibid 13). This period of progress was stalled in 1914 but re-emerged after the world wars, culminating in the globalization period or "global village" as per the 1960 vernacular (ibid 15).

Indeed, the twentieth century was a violent one, particularly when compared to the nineteenth century. Hobsbawm reasons that there was excellent material progress during this relatively stable period known as Pax Britannica (British peace). The Concert of Europe brought about this peace as an international regime (Keohane 1984; Krasner 1983); the Concert of Europe met to maintain the balance of power. The balance of power ensured that no power could gain more military power and international influence than any other power. In this sense, the great powers coordinated their foreign policies to tamp down any one state's ambition. For instance, if the Russians were to gain from a quick victory against the Ottoman Empire, then other powers such as Great Britain and France would step in for the Ottoman Empire to neutralize Russian ambitions. In this sense, a state's thirst for power could be curbed, and wars remained limited. This international system, even in its multipolar form, was inherently stable, except for moments when the balance of power had to shift, such as in the Crimean War above.

Essentially, the international system established by the Concert of Europe was stable as no state wanted to repeat the first Napoleonic Wars. There were several coalition wars to prevent France from ruling the entire continent. Indeed, France was a continental force that prevailed even as many rival states outnumbered it. It is interesting then to see that people base their opinions on the horrors of past wars.

Hobsbawm's description of the nineteenth century is juxtaposed with the twentieth century. He states that any wars or conflicts in the nineteenth century were short, fought in weeks or months and not years (Hobsbawm 1994, 23). Fighting was restricted to those who agreed to fight. War deaths were limited to combatants in the tens or hundreds of thousands rather than the millions (ibid 24). Thus, the size and scope of the war were vastly different in the nineteenth century than in the twentieth in terms of deaths and geographic area.

Like the nineteenth-century emperors of the great powers of the Concert of Europe, it seems that twentieth-century academics based their understanding of the century on past wars. Seeing the scale of warfare and the destruction of human potential, Hobsbawm and his peers interpret the twentieth century as a horror.

Returning to the *Age of Extremes*, Hobsbawm begins chapter 1, entitled "Age of Total War," with a short description of the nineteenth century. He states that wars were limited to specific areas rather than world wars. He also adds that no world wars existed before the twentieth century (bid 23). However, this seems incorrect as Gilpin (1988) posits that several hegemonic wars impacted the international system. These wars are the Thirty Years' War (Gilpin 1988, 606) and the Napoleonic Wars (ibid 608). The Seven Years' War might also be included. These wars involved many of the great powers of the era and were fought in various theaters around the world to control the international system. However, I believe Hobsbawm's point is that there were no world wars in the nineteenth century; indeed, no war outside its region.

The limited scope of war described above might have impacted European leaders' perception of war and its conduct. The past does have an impact on the shaping of expectations. After a long century of limited and relatively quick warfare, coupled with technological innovations that encouraged offense over defense (van Evera 1998), it influenced ideas of quick victory and limited war. The infamous Schlieffen Plan is an ideal physical manifestation of these attitudes; a quick German victory against the French would then move troops and resources on the Eastern front leading to a quick Triple Entente defeat.

Of course, World War I was anything but quick. Battle deaths soared in the millions. Hobsbawm argues that the conflict began as a European conflict and extended outward into colonies, encouraging other actors to enter the fray for territorial gain (Hobsbawm 1994, 24). The past created these expectations, but so did technology (or lack thereof) that made such feats theoretically possible. As a result, it seems that there was a misperception of war that resulted from the peaceful nineteenth century: that wars would be limited to specific areas and that any war would be over in months or weeks and not years. This gross misperception led to World War I and four years of destruction.

The destruction of death that followed the four years of World War I managed to shift perceptions of war. The veterans emerged fundamentally against the very idea of war (ibid 26). Politicians also understood that the voting public would never again stand for such conflict (ibid). The very people initially enthusiastic about war and conflict, including many on the political left, were turned off by the very idea. The willingness to do whatever it took to avoid war was reflected by the welcoming of British appeasement to Hitler's annexation of parts of Czechoslovakia and even before then with German remilitarization. The driver of conflict that led to World War II could be levied upon the fascist movements across Europe. It was not a product of nationalist yet democratic European states that hoped for quick gains and glory. However, this did not mean that the victors of World War I had little responsibility for World War II. The victors of World War I played an essential role in defining the perceptions of war and the ramifications of losing a war.

The Triple Entente alliance played an essential role in defining war length. Rather than suing for peace, both sides decided it would be in their best interest to continue to war regardless of the costs brought on by the apparent stalemate (ibid 29–30). Continuing the war was better than calling for an armistice; the idea of complete surrender was the only factor to be considered. Hobsbawm calls this an "absurd and self-defeating aim which ruined both victors and vanquished" (ibid 30). Once total war achieved a complete victory against Germany, Austria-Hungary, and the Ottoman Empire, losing states were forced to sign harsh treaties. Germany, in particular, was forced to accept a war-guilt clause that was considered unfair. The reparations forced upon Germany were particularly destructive, leading to periods of economic instability and facilitating the rise of Adolph Hitler. The international system created in the post-World War I era was a political and economic system engineered to keep Germany weak. Keeping Germany down was fundamental to constructing the new international system defined by the tremendous victorious powers, specifically France and Great Britain. The United States was also an essential member of Woodrow Wilson's advancement of the League of Nations, specifically notions of self-determination and sovereignty. This particular development was relegated to the background, as power politics still determined international political outcomes such as the Treaty of Versailles.

The twentieth-century international system was very different compared to the international system of the nineteenth century. One significant difference was the nature of the system. As mentioned, the nineteenth-century international system was determined by a fluid alliance system to maintain a balance of power. Hence, alliances shifted on a case-by-case basis. It became more static over time culminating in World War I, but ultimately the Concert of Europe was based on the mutual recognition of great power status and prestige. Maintaining an equal and stable balance of power could prevent prolonged war. After World War I, the twentieth-century international system was based not on a Concert of Europe or mutual recognition of power but on a unipolar balance of power. Unipolarity means that one power (or alliance thereof) would determine international political outcomes for all other members, including competitors. The Treaty of Versailles was one such part of the system that punished Germany and the other losers of World War I. This punishment was to maintain German weakness and the supremacy of France and Great Britain. Hence, the international systems of the different eras were considerably different.

As discussed, the post-World War I international system and perceptions of warfare were very different from the nineteenth century. However, there were similarities in that the international system generated specific types of conflict. To Hobsbawm, the international system in the nineteenth century produced wars for economic purposes. These conflicts were primarily to gain access to markets to increase economic growth, bolstering competitiveness (ibid 29). He calls this particular century the "Age of Empire" due to the fusion of economics and politics. This notion gave no limit to warfare. World War I was thus a conflict similar to Gilpin's hegemonic war (1988) "since Germany wanted a global political and maritime position like that now occupied by Britain and which therefore would automatically relegate an already declining Britain to an inferior status" (ibid 30). Thus, for Great Britain, the way to defend its position was to drive Germany into a humiliating defeat so that it may never rise again to challenge the British international system (ibid). Having survived the war, the British international system was to continue, however, not with the same power as before. The war completely ruined the economy and pushed the state beyond its capability.

Hobsbawm argues that the international system (although he never uses the term) was never the same after the war, that "total victory ratified by the penal, dictated peace, ruined what little chances there were of restoring something even faintly like a stable, liberal, bourgeois Europe …" (ibid 30). However, if we understand the international system to be one where economics and politics are fused, there are some similarities. German reparations are just one example of this, as money had to be paid to the Allies. Reparations were an economic tool to keep Germany weak, even creating German dependence on the United States and other powers to maintain some standard of living and political sovereignty (cite Marxist literature on dependence). For instance, to pay reparations, Germany had to take out loans from the United States. When this failed, France invaded Germany and occupied the Ruhr. France was determined to get its money. In other instances as well, the empires of the nineteenth century continued to exist. France and Great Britain still had control over their colonies, and these colonies existed to keep colonial powers wealthy.

In summary, the nineteenth-century's international system differed significantly from the twentieth century. The old Concert of Europe and balance of power arrangement that kept Europe in relative peace for ninety-nine years (1815–1914) was traded in for a much bolder, British, and French-dominated Europe at the expense of Germany. However, the international systems were also similar due to the fusion of political-economic foundations. The end of World War I brought a shift in the previous perception of war as a concise and contained way to settle conflicts of state interests. It was hoped that the world would be at peace by keeping an aggressor down. Of course, Great Britain ceased to be the powerhouse it once was. Indeed, the British Empire, as it was pre-World War I, did not survive the war; the problem was that the mentality and self-esteem of the British Empire failed to acknowledge this vast reduction in power. Since its power did not carry over after the war, it can be argued that Great Britain failed to survive and thus lost World War I in its way. This became even more obvious during World War II when Great Britain began to play second fiddle to the much more powerful United States and the Soviet Union. Indeed, it took eleven years during the Suez Crisis for Britain to ultimately acknowledge its secondary, middle-power role in the international system.

Hobsbawm notes that Germany harbored resentment against the states of the Triple Entente for the humiliating Treaty of Versailles (ibid 36). He states,

> Dissatisfaction with the status quo was not confined to the defeated states, although these, and notably Germany, felt they had plenty of cause for resentment, as indeed was the case. Every party in Germany, from the Communists on the left to Hitler's National Socialists on the extreme right, concurred in condemning the Versailles Treaty as unjust and unacceptable.
>
> (ibid)

This peace treaty served as the foundation of the international system and was based on the humiliation of Germany. A reinvigorated Germany would soon overturn the international system. I assume no one understood the speed at which such an endeavor would be attempted. It was only ten years after the occupation of the Ruhr when Hitler took power. The motivating factor that drove the rise of Hitler was fundamentally a psychological one; Germans simply could not accept the status of humiliation that was placed upon them by foreign powers that were just as guilty of the war.

Germany was one power that was against the international system's status quo. Another state, the Soviet Union, was opposed to it, as were Japan and Italy. War was seen as a means by which the status quo could be overthrown and the system recreated (ibid 37). Hobsbawm states that "the states that were drawn into the war against these three [Germany, Japan, and Italy], whether capitalist or socialist, did not want a war, and most of them did what they could to avoid one" (ibid 36). It is difficult to accept that the Soviet Union simply did not want war, specifically in a systemic sense. The Soviet Union was considered a rogue force and was never entirely accepted by status quo European powers. The Russian Civil War reflected this notion, as many Western states sent volunteers to fight on the side of conservative monarchists. The Soviet Union cannot be considered part of the Western capitalist world but a force well enough on its own. Led by Joseph Stalin, the Soviet Union pursued its revisionist interests, including, most notably, being a signatory to the Molotov-Ribbentrop Non-aggression Pact. This idea of non-aggression is a misnomer used to conceal the truth of the matter: the pact led to the invasion and, ultimately, the partition and annexation of Poland. Hence, the Soviet Union did not want war as much as it did not want to fight with Germany. By enabling Nazi Germany to fight against Western powers and taking on a systemic position, one can see that the only victor in any war would be the state that sat on the sidelines: the Soviet Union. This was truer in the case of the United States, which did not join the war until 1941. Until then, it would sell weapons and equipment to Great Britain and gain substantial power from that relationship (ibid 48). Hence, the primary systemic victor in any war would be the states that stay out of the conflict while others bleed themselves white. Hobsbawm notes that "a Second World War ... would ruin the British economy, and disband large parts of the British Empire" (ibid 154).

It is important to note that Great Britain understood that Hitler had designs on the international system. Hobsbawm argued that Great Britain and Germany abandoned the realpolitik that defined previous eras. Instead, both parties realized the war would have to be fought sooner or later, and this war would repeat World War I: long, drawn out, and expensive (ibid). However, World War II did not start in 1939; it began in 1936 with the onset of the Spanish Civil War, which lasted until 1939.

To Hobsbawm, the Spanish Civil War was "the quintessential expression of global confrontation" (ibid 156). He argues that even though Francisco Franco, head of the Phalange, was labeled a "fascist," he cannot be described as such (ibid). However, Hitler and Mussolini would fund his side against the clumsy amalgam of anarchist, socialist, communist, and other republican fighters funded by the Soviet Union,

France, and Great Britain. Hobsbawm calls this a global confrontation because it was a significant manifestation of the international competition between Great Britain and Germany. The Spanish Civil War is what would eventually become known as a proxy war. A proxy war is a war that shows an indirect connection between significant powers seeking to bolster a local ally without getting directly involved in the conflict. One cannot study the Spanish Civil War thoroughly without taking note of this international aspect. It signals great power competition and forms a significant signpost of the uneasiness between great powers that form the international system. Thus a proxy war is directly connected to the hegemonic struggle that great powers find themselves in as they battle for systemic supremacy. The weapons provided by the great power sponsors also served as a proving ground to see which weapons were superior. It was not simply a test of power but a comprehensive test of strength. This competition would lead to the undoing of the international system, as Hitler moved to destroy the Treaty of Versailles and make Germany a continental power at the expense of the status quo.

The economic and technological position of states during the war, mainly systemic or hegemonic, can advance if the mobilization of those resources is used to advance their position in the system in the post-war environment. In many ways, war can be used to advance economic growth. However, that growth is artificial if states do not prepare for the following peace. As World War II progressed, it became necessary for the Allies to prepare for a post-war environment. The compromises that followed, such as the percentages agreement, and the Tehran, Yalta, and Potsdam conferences, would usher in a new international system governed by two central states: the United States and the Soviet Union.

The International System from the Twentieth to the Twenty-first Century

The collapse of the British/French international system that dominated until 1939 signaled a new beginning. No longer would hegemony be from Europe, but rather from across the pond. The United States was now the state that underwrote the international system for much of the world. There was also the Soviet Union that now had control over all of Eastern Europe and much of Central Europe to the German city of Berlin. As a result, a bipolar system emerged that placed the United

States on one end of the spectrum and the Soviet Union at the other. It was a military and political confrontation but also one with a foundation in economic systems: the free market system of the United States versus the Soviet Union's socialist system. In many ways, the challenge stemmed from the Russian Civil War that started in 1917 to 1922, fought between the White Conservative Monarchists and leftist forces of the Reds. Hobsbawm notes that the Reds won partly due to their slogan of "Bread, Peace, and Land" (1995, 61). Conservative forces simply could not sell their ideas to a peasant class interested in self-preservation. Peasants and other poorer groups could not buy into the royalist system. The Soviet Union in 1945 then made it clear that its interests were about liberating the world's poor from systems of exploitation. Hobsbawm describes that "universal emancipation, the construction of a better alternative to capitalist society was, after all, its fundamental reason for existence [the Soviet Union's]" (ibid 72). This is why the Soviets were involved in conflicts worldwide: to protect similar working-class movements and thus lead the world into a new socialist century. The United States saw the Soviet Union as an inherent threat to its way of life.

The United States understood the threat of international socialism and appreciated that various political and economic systems grew in prominence after the Great Depression (1929). Consequently, many knew that capitalism in its laissez-faire form could not continue to exist. The post-war period was an economic system that synthesized domestic security and a balance of power in the bipolar Cold War arrangement. This is true for both the United States and the Soviet Union. Each power had to show that its economic system was superior and should be adopted by other states, especially those newly independent states in the international system. This explains the competition for weak states, as expressed by the multitude of proxy wars and superpower interventions during this time. While it was in no way peaceful for weak states, there was no large-scale and direct confrontation between the superpowers: only through their proxies. There was a balance of power arrangement with battles for dominance in the developing world. There was still competition in the 1950s and 1960s. Economically, the capitalist-socialist dialectic resulted in a managed form of capitalism we understand as Keynesianism.

The Golden Age of Capitalism lasted from the 1950s way into the 1960s and was a period of relatively low inflation, low unemployment, and a high standard of living. This is considered the Golden

Age because it successfully grew the middle class in the United States, Europe, and other countries worldwide. However, changes in the global economic system would change the political system again. Global competition from Japan and Europe, combined with the inflation caused by the increased cost of production (wages), OPEC, and a severe rate of decline in productivity growth, all united against the American economy and the very concept of capitalism. Specifically, the very structure of the Golden Age system was creating the burdens that perpetuated the crisis. In other words, the success of the Golden Age could not be sustained over the long term. These alterations also changed society as urbanization brought more vital unions, increasing wages, lower profits, and soon inflation. Thus, increased wages did play an integral role at the end of the Golden Ages. However, the very structures of capitalism, and the reliance on continued expansion, would have eventually been curtailed. Hence, like the Soviet system, the American golden age had to end to be replaced by a more laissez-faire policy. This policy would come to define the unipolar era of the international system led by the United States.

Like the nineteenth century, the twentieth century saw this fusion of economic and political systems described by Hobson (2005) and Hobsbawm (1994). Hegemonic competition is thus defined as a battle for systems. Economic systems form a significant part of this confrontation, as described previously in the theoretical section. Economic growth leads to military and political power, leading to further demands on the existing political system. When the Soviet Union collapsed, the United States could recreate the system and did so, in part, through its international economic institutions, such as the International Monetary Fund. To borrow, developing states must adopt specific liberal principles and reforms. This creates a dependency on the United States due to the destructive nature of reforms. The international system has led to severe economic gains for all states, including China.

In the final chapter, Hobsbawm seeks to understand the international order in post-Soviet power. He begins this chapter lamenting the lack of a balance of power. He states:

... for the first time in two centuries, the world of the 1990s entirely lacked any international system or structure. The fact that, after 1989, dozens of new territorial states appeared without any mechanism for determining their borders—without even third parties

accepted as sufficiently impartial to act as general mediators—
speaks for itself.

(ibid 559)

It is unclear from the chapter if Hobsbawm is using the notion of
systems and structures here as it relates to Structural Realist theory.
However, putting this aside, he points to the fact that the newly independent states met no opposition from the Soviet Union or Russia: such
developments were simply accepted as the new political reality. The
only great power that managed to survive intact and strengthened
was the United States (ibid). The old empires were now long gone,
swept into the dustbin of history. However, the new political reality
did reflect the nineteenth century: the emergence of one great power
with the ability to set the political agenda for others; Pax Britannica of
the nineteenth century was now Pax Americana.

Due to the fusion of politics and economics, a new political-
economic reality also emerged naturally: the re-emergence of laissez-
faire economic systems in the Washington Consensus. There were
no other competitors in the United States. While Japan and Germany
had some latent potential, they did not have political clout. While the
Soviet Union formerly had political and economic clout, its economic
collapse destroyed its capacity for global political ambition (ibid 574).
There were thus no challenges to the American order except from violent non-state actors such as nationalist militant groups and terrorist
organizations (ibid 560–561). Thus, the international system became
one governed by the forces of capitalism pushed on by major international economic institutions of the IMF and WTO.

From this, Hobsbawm sees the international system after the Soviet
Union's collapse as one of disorder (ibid 562). The United States
sought to increase its economic system but did not provide political
guidance or order. He calls this "impotence" that refused to manage
the political order. There was no longer embedded liberalism of the
Golden Age but rather a push to disembed and further liberalize the
political economy. Since there was no challenge from the Soviet
Union, as Marxism had failed to provide the good life, the United
States could relax its efforts. Thus, replacing the international system
was a non-system led by the invisible hand of a new global laissez-
faire society (bid 564). Such was a revolution as even the British
laissez-faire system was organized under a stable currency regime of
the silver standard.

To Hobsbawm, this very recognition of the supremacy of capitalism in its most disembedded form led to the perspective that the nation-state and realist thinking were no longer helpful. Since there were no more state-centric threats, there was no use for state-centric theories (ibid 574; 576). As Hobsbawm notes,

By the end of the century, the nation-state was on the defensive against a world economy it could not control; against the institutions it had constructed to remedy its international weakness, such as the European Union; against its apparent financial incapacity to maintain the services to its citizens.

(ibid 556–557)

Hobsbawm then argues that this system lacked an authority figure. Unlike many American intellectuals like Francis Fukuyama, who saw the victory of capitalism and democracy, Hobsbawm saw confusion and instability (Hobsbawm 1994, 580).

Hobsbawm ends the book by warning readers about the destabilizing effects of unrestrained capitalism (ibid 584). He states:

The structures of human societies, including even some of the social foundations of the capitalist economy, are destroyed by the erosion of what we inherited from the human past. Our world risks both explosion and implosion ... if humanity is to have a recognizable future, it cannot be by prolonging the past or the present. If we try to build the third millennium on that basis, we shall fail. Moreover, the price of failure, the alternative to a changed society, is darkness.

(ibid 584–585)

Hobsbawm ends his book in a very pessimistic way. It is diametrically opposite to American thinkers like Francis Fukuyama and Thomas Friedman. In many respects, this could be because of Hobsbawm's Marxist approach. However, I think such thinking is quite pretentious. As a historian, Hobsbawm synthesizes large swaths of historical data and extracts repeated patterns of behavior. This chapter describes some major repetition points that emerged during that time.

The first aspect to discuss is the implosion of the American century's economic system. The 2008 Financial Crisis almost collapsed the international economic system. The laissez-faire system that led to the mortgage crisis was a manifestation of unbridled capitalism. The assumption of rationality that every investor makes their decisions was found faulty, as irrational exuberance led people to take on mortgages they could not pay back, led banks to allow those people to take mortgages, and led investors to use enormous amounts of leverage to buy junk mortgage-backed securities for maximum profit. Thus, similar to the Great Depression in 1929, eighty-nine years later, the same irrational exuberance gave way to a total economic collapse. However, unlike in 1929, the United States bailed out many of these so-called "too big to fail" entities and took on large amounts of debt, leading to an angry public reaction on both the political left and right.

In many instances, a liberalized economy wrought significant winners and losers. The unbridled economy brought on by the North American Treaty Organization and the inclusion of China in the World Trade Organization allowed Mexico and China opportunities to grow at the expense of American industry. The fusion of economic and political influence led to the political rise of China. Scholars tried to express this development in the states versus markets debate.

States versus Markets: The Crux of the Post-Cold War Debate[1]

To understand the period in question, from the end of the Cold War to 9/11, it is necessary to study and reflect on the literature that defined this particular period. Many of these works were primarily predictive. Scholars assumed that if specific trends continued, the international order would no longer be dominated by states but by several actors. Forces of globalization would be the primary driver of this transformation. However, to base an opinion on trends and certainty that such movements would continue forever is wrong-headed. Investors in the stock market might make decisions based on trends but must be aware that specific developments are tenuous and potentially temporary.

In the late 1990s and early 2000s, scholars (to be discussed) began to perceive a fundamental change in the international order. The debate was between those academics who thought that globalization was destroying the state while others argued that the state was still the most important actor. Globalization can be defined as

a process (or set of processes) which embodies a transformation in the spatial organization of social relations and transactions— assessed in terms of their extensity, intensity, velocity, and impact—generating transcontinental or interregional flows and networks of activity, interaction and the exercise of power.

(Held et al. 1999, 15)

According to the latter part of the definition, the state is no longer the unit wielding state power. Markets—another competing force—are the primary driver of power. Is globalization weakening, strengthening, or transforming state power? This article will argue that the state is and continues to be resilient due to the preeminence of energy and global influence. This was not always the case. The literature posits several explanations, which will now be discussed briefly. Throughout these works, note that power (military power) is not considered a vital force that shapes world order but rather the force of the market. This change in attitude can be articulated further by Keohane and Nye when they described complex interdependence:

1 Multiple channels connect societies, including informal ties between governmental elites and formal foreign office arrangements, informal ties among nongovernmental elites (face-to-face and through telecommunications), and transnational organizations (such as multinational banks or corporations) ...

2 The agenda of interstate relationships consists of multiple issues that are not arranged in a clear or consistent hierarchy. This absence of hierarchy among issues means, among other things, that military security does not consistently dominate the agenda ...

3 Military force is not used by governments toward other regional governments or on issues when complex interdependence prevails ... Military force could, for instance, be irrelevant to resolving disagreements in economic matters ... (1989, 20–21).

From this, globalization scholars (Frankel 2000; Strange 1988; Cerny 1994) argue that state interests are pushed aside in favor of the market.

Frankel (2000) states that globalization and the withering away of the state have brought about fundamental systemic changes within the international system, stemming from two primary sources: increased modes of communication brought about by technology and increased economic integration since World War II. These innovations have brought states and their destinies together: they have more in common and act similarly. Further, Friedman (1999) notes that increased market interaction impacts a state's public goods and services provision. In its attempt to embrace the advantages of globalization, the state must pull on the golden straitjacket, elusively promising considerable wealth to its participants while limiting the independence of an actor. Taxes and interest rates must be maintained to ensure the full participation of multinational corporations and investors. Otherwise, a state could lose out on such gains. Dollar and Kraay (2004) take a different perspective on the declining nature of the state. According to the Stolper-Samuelson model, free trade allows factor prices, including wages, to converge. The state no longer has the authority to set salaries in any sense. Instead, the model would point to increased wages because of free trade. They look to Vietnam and note that the population living under $1 a day has decreased dramatically.

Adding to this discussion is Susan Strange (1988; 1996), who looks at the declining relevancy of the state in international markets. She argues that the state no longer controls itself; the markets dominate and define agendas. Some non-state actors have become more powerful than states as the see-saw of power plays in favor of the former. In England, the Black Wednesday of the 1990s proved this as the state tried to maintain the pound's value as speculators attacked it like George Soros. Billions of dollars were lost that day as it became clear that the state could no longer set the agenda.

With regard to the power of the state over economic policy (economic sovereignty), Cerny (1994) takes the conversation toward the welfare state. Cerny posits that the state reconfigured its priorities from focusing on welfare and providing public goods and services to address the issues stemming from an unstable global economic environment toward a more competitive market-oriented system. The state and its government are no longer accountable to the people but to the investor. The state must therefore create an environment using its fiscal and monetary policy to ensure its viability for global business.

Giddens (2003) argues in "Runaway World" that increased technologies have brought about a world where people and states are brought closer together by technology, so much so that states do not have control over much. Hardt and Negri (2000) take on a more critical, Neo-Marxist and Foucauldian approach, detailing the destruction of sovereignty by the world market as fundamentally a form of biopower that defines legitimacy. Any action that offends the market is illegitimate and will result in the destruction and isolation of that state.

The previous scholars seem to agree that global markets are overcoming the power and sovereignty of the state. Of course, some scholars (to follow) disagree with these assessments and argue that there is no so-called Race to the Bottom (RTB) as described above. The competing arguments, in some cases, are from transformationalists, while other positions are taken from statists and institutionalists. McGrew and Held (2002) argue that the state is still relevant, although globalization and its benefits are integral to the welfare of many people. They argue that the state is being transformed from its traditional self, one characterized by sovereignty and security, to one functioning under the ideals of liberal internationalism. The state is consequently more engaged in the world, seeking to solve global problems and market failures within international institutions. This is important for legitimacy, as it encourages the participation of people within borders, not forgetting the people the market is supposed to serve. Keohane and Martin (1995) take on the same argument by underscoring these transformations; however, reminding us that the world is made up of people. Taking a classical realist perspective, they state that anarchy still exists, that is, the Hobbesian state system is still present. Thus, sovereignty and security remain important, even as trade and financial integration continue to unite the world. Slaughter (2000) is another scholar who disagrees with the "Race to the Bottom" hypothesis. She argues that the idea is invalid due to its faulty conception of the state and continues advocating for the relevancy of the state. Furthermore, she promotes a bureaucratic method of global governance called transgovernmentalism, seeking to address problems concerning all states. She points to the Clinton era and his use of bureaucrats to solve global issues.

Other authors refuse to adhere to the state's eulogy. Scholars (Waltz 1999; Gilpin 2001) continue prioritizing state actors and institutions, maintaining their significance in the age of globalization. Two main perspectives harken from Realist perspectives of International Political Economy and liberal and institutional approaches. First to be discussed are the Realist arguments of Waltz (1999) and Gilpin (2001). Waltz argues that globalization is a product of the Hegemonic Stability Theory; the only reason the world operates within a liberal economic framework is because of the state and the actions of the most powerful state.

According to the Hegemonic Stability Theory, first formulated by Kindleberger (1973), globalization exists because it is in the interest of the most powerful state, the United States, which continues to be dominant even throughout the decline of the Bretton Woods System. Waltz also points out that globalization seems limited among allies and Northern Latitudes, meaning that the international system and security concerns persist. Gilpin argues in concurrence with these perspectives but adds that globalization is indeed reversible and vulnerable to wars of the hegemonic variety. Foreign Direct Investment (FDI) is also inherently political because of concerns for survival. Multinational Corporations and other actors considered equal to the state is a false notion. Instead, they must operate within the context of state rules and regulations.

Globalization's unraveling began to be discussed seriously after the 2008 financial crisis. This is because globalization's hegemon, the United States, suffered a significant economic shock the world over. Altman (2009) points out that globalization is indeed reversible. He points out that the recent financial crisis has affected the more deregulated and liberal states like the United States. These vulnerabilities have been passed on to other nations interconnected with the United States and the SIC PIGS (Slovenia, Ireland, Cyprus, Portugal, Italy, Greece, and Spain). This not only delegitimizes the liberal way of globalization but has enhanced the state capitalism system of BRICS. Small states will look to the BRICS for their state-led strategies and lessen the influence of the liberal powers, thus making the so-called RTB reversible. From another perspective, Rodrik's (1998) argument of "more trade, more government" is also increasingly relevant during these tumultuous times. He argues that the more integrated a state becomes within the global economy, the more it will benefit. Simultaneously, that state will become more affected by the ups and downs of the worldwide economy. Seeing this, labor will demand protection from this flux through organization and protest. Thus, regardless of increased international trade and financial ties, the state still mattered as a political entity that maintained a barrier with the outside world.

To summarize, much of the Post-Cold War literature discussed here concerned the declining relevance of the state when compared to either market forces or people power. Globalization was the new buzzword discussed in both a positive and negative light. However, the state and national security issues remained constant. Indeed, there were several moments of genuine concern that states with significant power capability could go to war. Throughout the 1990s and early

2000s, NATO expanded to include members of the post-Soviet space. Russia outrightly rejected this development as a threat to its existence and prestige. The Third Taiwan Strait Crisis (1995–1996) also saw significant American power projection in East Asia in response to China's missile tests inside Taiwan's territorial waters. There were also significant concerns about Russia and China's NATO bombing of Serbia; the latter saw its embassy bombed in 1999.

In retrospect, it was clear that state-centric security still mattered to significant power regardless of the ability of market forces and other trends of the era. Attention to non-state issues, especially after 9/11, served to discredit military focus. During this period, realist thought was seemingly marginalized by wider academia; as Mearsheimer (2002, 23) writes:

> Many Americans and Europeans, however, believe that realism has a dim future. With the end of the Cold War, as the argument goes, international politics changed in fundamental ways. The world has not simply moved from bipolarity to multipolarity. Still, instead, we have entered an era where there is little prospect of security competition among the great powers, not to mention the war, and where concepts such as polarity and the balance of power matter little for understanding international relations. Most states now view each other as members of an emerging "international community," not as potential military rivals. Opportunities for cooperation are abundant in this new world, and the result will likely be increased prosperity and peace for almost all the states in the system.

World politics have changed, and realist theory has been proved obsolescent to be shelved, as Thomas Kuhn suggests in *The Structure of Scientific Revolutions* (1996). Mearsheimer adds: "…to proponents of this optimistic perspective … realism is old thinking and largely irrelevant to the new realities of world politics. Realists have gone the way of the dinosaurs; they do not realize it" (ibid 23–24). The article describes the animosity toward realist thought but also ends with a sort of warning: "Realism will disappear only if there is a revolutionary change in the structure of the international system, but that is not likely to happen anytime soon" (ibid 31). Writing in 2002, Mearsheimer probably understood that the unipolar system would soon change to a bipolar or multipolar system, especially if the United States did what great powers usually do: overextend themselves

(Kennedy 1987). Nineteen years later, it seems this is indeed the case (to be discussed). It would certainly seem that the international system is now multipolar especially given the rise of China.

Chinese growth rates increased to such an extent that many now argue that it will soon overtake the United States. However, this issue ignores the economic-political fusion already at play. China already heads major international economic institutions directly challenging the United States, such as the New Development Bank (Pederson 2014). China also operates at the bilateral level, granting loans to developing states without strings attached. Developing states often cannot repay these loans, forcing them to surrender the sovereignty of various parts of their state to China. Some examples include:

- In 2011, China reportedly agreed to write off an unknown amount of debt owed by Tajikistan in exchange for some 1,158 square kilometers of the disputed territory. At the time, Tajik authorities said they only agreed to provide 5.5 percent of the land that Beijing sought initially.
- In 2011, with Cuba in a desperate economic situation and seeking debt relief, China, its largest single creditor, agreed to restructure between $4–6 billion of the debt. The details of the transaction were not disclosed, but it reportedly included an agreement by China to extend additional trade credits and financing for port rehabilitation. Some recent reports indicate that some of the debt was forgiven.
- With Sri Lanka unwilling to service a $1.1 billion package of loans to China, with interest rates ranging from 2 to 6.3 percent, to finance the construction of the Hambantota Port, the two countries agreed to an arrangement whereby China transferred funds equivalent to the loan amount ($1.1 billion) to the Sri Lankan government in exchange for an 85 percent equity stake in the port company under a ninety-nine-year concession (Hurley et al. 2018, 20).

China also uses its wealth to buy critical European ports (Kakissis 2018). China now owns stakes in ports in Greece, Belgium, France, The Netherlands, Spain, Italy, Malta, and Turkey and stakes in Egypt and Morocco (ibid). Many in the European Union are increasingly concerned about this perceived encirclement as Theresa Fallon, a China analyst in Brussels, argues that China may gain a political foothold in Europe that could potentially limit European Union autonomy and sovereignty:

There is a phrase, "pre-emptive obedience," that is often used to discuss relations with the Chinese ... It means making decisions with the idea of not upsetting China. That is already happening, worrying if you consider the stakes. If you think of China's growth strategy [in maritime ports], they have invested all along the peripheries of Europe. So it is like an anaconda strategy: Surround it and squeeze it.

(Fallon quoted in ibid)

There are also severe political and military concerns associated with the rise of China. China is seeking to overturn the international system in many respects, like Nazi Germany and the German Empire before it. In many respects, China no longer respects or wants to be hemmed in by the status quo international system. The first aspect is the destruction of Hong Kong's autonomy. China has defined an agreement with the United Kingdom to let Hong Kong remain autonomous until 2047. This is due to the new national security law that blurred the lines between the two areas. China also does not respect the ruling from the Hague regarding the South China Sea. It has ignored the Hague ruling that refuses China's demand for control over all of the South China Sea. Further and most worrisome for the stability of the international system is China's constant demands to annex Taiwan. It has also interned millions of Uighur Muslims in internment camps and has turned Uighur cities into veritable open-air prisons.

From this, we can see that there are clear, repeated patterns of behavior that create international systems. The wealthier a state becomes, the more likely that state seeks to overturn the international system. The fusion of economic and political systems is the foundation of this destructive behavior. However, given the historical narrative expressed by Hobsbawm, it is altogether expected. Another significant feature, proxy wars, has continued into our new century. Proxy wars are a significant signpost of hegemonic confrontation.

Proxy wars are also a significant feature that continued into the bipolar Cold War system and the multipolarity of today's system. As argued, the Spanish Civil War signaled the beginning of a broader systemic confrontation between great powers: Nazi Germany and Great Britain. In the Cold War, proxy conflicts involved one great power. The Vietnam War, the Korean War, the Soviet invasion of Afghanistan, the Lebanese Civil War, and the wars in Central America can all be considered wars by proxy. Indeed, the Cold War was cold because the involvement of great powers limited it. In today's system, we also see the rise of proxy wars, especially in weaker states. Saudi Arabia (backed by the United States) and Iran (backed by China and Russia) are fighting proxy wars in Yemen, Iraq, Lebanon, and Syria. Ukraine is another example as the United States sides with the Ukrainian government while Russia is more actively involved, siding with the Russian minority there. The developing situation in Myanmar, specifically the military coup there, could be financed by China to gain further access to Myanmar's seaports, thereby circumventing the Straits of Malacca. In many ways, the legacy of the Spanish Civil War continues today.

How do the perceptions of the Twentieth Century impact and shape our understanding of international politics and the conduct of war, more specifically, systemic war, today? One of the first notations from Hobsbawm is the idea that war has become impersonal (Hobsbawm 1994, 50). In World War I, trench warfare demanded that soldiers get "up close and personal" with those killed. Technology began to change this aspect of conflict (however, similar brutalities continue). Specifically, World War II marked a new beginning. Hobsbawm writes:

> … the new impersonality of warfare, which turned to kill and to maim into the remote consequence of pushing a button or moving a lever. Technology made its victims invisible, as people eviscerated by bayonets or seen through the sights of firearms could not be.
>
> (ibid)

In many ways today, we see what Hobsbawm describes as the "operational necessity" of collateral damage through the impersonality of drone strikes. One recent strike launched by the Biden administration in 2021 demonstrates the impersonality of such attacks. General Mark Milley describes this impersonality:

> We know from the variety of other means that at least one of those killed was an ISIS facilitator … Were there others killed? Yes, there are others killed. Who they are, we do not know. We will try to sort through all that. However, we believe that the procedures at this point—I do not want to influence the outcome of an investigation—but at this point, we think that procedures were correctly followed. It was a righteous strike.
>
> (Milley quoted in Kheel 2021)

This idea of a *righteous strike* should stand out, as even though unknowns were killed in this particular incident, it was an operational necessity. The terrible aspect is that the people killed in this particular incident were charity workers (Romo 2021). In many respects, this attitude has defined much of the conduct of war, as war is seen as a regrettable but natural part of the international system. The Civil War in Yemen, the most destructive proxy war, and the world's most alarming humanitarian crisis continue to this day. It remains an expression of great power conflict even while the international system depends on the free exchange of goods and services within the norm of globalization.

Conclusions

The nineteenth century seemed to Hobsbawm a relatively peaceful century that ultimately failed and produced what he and others consider the worst century ever. While there has been significant progress in the twentieth century with the advent of women's rights, LGBTQIA++ rights, workers' rights, environmental protections, and so forth, it seems that war and repeated economic collapse overshadowed these developments.

What prevents the world order from changing, given changes in the distribution of capabilities? Like World War II, there is much to lose if China, a revisionist power, seeks to replace status quo powers. The same can be said about the United States and its efforts to prevent or block China's rise. Other alarming issues signal the denigration of the international system. These stem from the central states constructing the international system's balance of power. First, there are severe internal issues in China. Currently, China is seeing a decrease in its economic performance stemming from the supposed impending collapse of its property markets. Xi Jinping recently reined in the debt-driven investment of mortgage companies, leading to companies almost defaulting on loans. Property values are expected to decrease, which means that properties once used as collateral for new loans may no longer be a viable strategy. This, coupled with a proposed property tax, may decrease housing prices. Since the housing market is estimated to be worth $55 trillion, it will be difficult to bail out. An economic collapse of this magnitude will undoubtedly have global effects.

The future of the United States also seems uncertain. It has taken on far too much debt, and its quantitative easing strategy may result in inflation and economic collapse. Like China, this will have global effects. There are also significant issues with Russia and Iran that point to overextension. Regime security is also a severe problem, as the January 6 attack on the American Congress shows the illegitimacy of government and elections long proclaimed by not just Donald Trump after 2020 but Hillary Clinton after 2016. Such a lack of confidence in the electoral system may result in further political violence as its legitimacy is continually questioned.

While these internal problems can potentially destroy the international economic system, excellent power confrontation remains a significant concern. As described, the political-economic fusion of state power results in systemic competition and, in many instances, world war. In many ways, the cycle is repeating itself. Hobsbawm's prediction (for lack of a better word) remains: if we do not change the conflictual process of the international political-economic system, we remain in impending collapse.

The world described above is very different from the one described by intellectuals, political scientists, and journalists in the 1990s. For optimists, the world was supposed to meet the climax of progress, the end of history: the victory of capitalism and democracy over authoritarianism. For others, state conflict would disappear, replaced by competing civilizations. Marxists would see a world of capitalist exploitation with no actual power center. These predictions did not come true. Chapter 3 will summarize this literature to better understand Politicism, the book's main proposed methodology.

Note

1 This section republishes part of the following work: Hanna Samir Kassab, "Globalization, Multipolarity, and Great Power Competition," (2023), published by Routledge, New York, (pages 11–15) reproduced with permission of Routledge.

References

Altman, R. (2009). Globalization in Retreat: Further Geopolitical Consequences of the Financial Crisis. *Foreign Affairs Online* www.foreignaffairs.com/articles/65153/roger-c-altman/globalization-in-retreat.

Cerny, P. (1994). The Dynamics of Financial Globalization: Technology, Market Structure, and Policy Response. *Policy Sciences*, *27*(4), 319–342.

Clausewitz, C. (1984). On War. In M. Howard, P. Paret, and B. Brodie (Eds.), Princeton University Press, Princeton.

Dollar, D. and Kraay, A. (2004). Trade, Growth, and Poverty. *The Economic Journal, 114*, F22–F49.

Frankel, J. (2000). *Globalization of the Economy* (August). NBER Working Paper No. w7858.

Friedman, T. (1999). *The Lexus and the Olive Tree*. Farrar, Straus, Giroux, New York.

Giddens, A. (2003). *Runaway World: How Globalisation Is Reshaping Our Lives*. Profile, London.

Gilpin, R. (1988). The Theory of Hegemonic War. *The Journal of Interdisciplinary History, 18*(4), 591–613.

Gilpin, R. (2001). *Global Political Economy: Understanding the International Economic Order*, Princeton University Press, Princeton.

Hardt, M. and Negri, A. (2000). *Empire*, Harvard University Press, Cambridge.

Held, D. A., McGrew, Goldblatt, D., and Perraton, J. (1999). *Global Transformations: Politics, Economics and Culture*, Stanford University Press, Stanford.

Hobsbawm, E. (1995). *Age of Extremes: The Short Twentieth Century 1914–1991*. Abacus, London.

Hobson, J. (2005). *Imperialism: A Study*. Cosimo, New York.

Hurley, J., Scott, M., and Portelance, G. (2018). Examining the Debt Implications of the Belt and Road Initiative from a Policy Perspective. *Center for Global Development,* accessed February 21, 2020, www.cgdev.org/sites/default/files/examining-debt-implications-belt-and-road-initiative-policy-perspective.pdf.

Kakissis, J. (2018). Chinese Firms Now Hold Stakes in over a Dozen European Ports. *NPR,* October 9, www.npr.org/2018/10/09/642587456/chinese-firms-now-hold-stakes-in-over-a-dozen-european-ports.

Kennedy, P. M. (1987). *The Rise and Fall of the Great Powers: Economic Change and Military Conflict from 1500 to 2000*, 1st ed. Random House, New York.

Keohane, R. and Martin, L. (1995). The Promise of Institutionalist Theory. *International Security, 20*(1), 39–51.

Keohane, Robert O. (1984). *After Hegemony: Cooperation and Discord in the World Political Economy*. Princeton University Press, Princeton.

Kheel, R. (2021). "General acknowledges 'others' killed in drone strike targeting ISIS car bomb." *The Hill,* September 1, 2021, accessed April 11, 2023 https://thehill.com/policy/defense/570402-top-general-acknowledges-others-killed-in-drone-strike-targeting-isis-car-bomb/.

Kindleberger, C. (1973). *The World in Depression, 1929–1939*. University of California Press, Berkeley.

Krasner, S. D. (1983). *International Regimes*, Cornell University Press, Ithaca.

Kuhn, T. (1996). *The Structure of Scientific Revolutions,* University of Chicago Press, Chicago.

Lasswell, H. (1936). *Politics: Who Gets What and When,* Whittlesey House, New York.

McGrew, A. and Held, D. (2002). *Governing Globalization: Power, Authority and Global Governance,* Wiley, Hoboken.

Mearsheimer, J. J. (2002). Realism, the Real World, and the Academy. In M. Brecher and F. P. Harvey (Eds.), *Realism and Institutionalism in International Studies* (pp. 23–33). University of Michigan Press, Ann Arbor.

Pederson, C. (2014). New Financing Options for Coal Power Plants through the BRICS 'New Development Bank.' *Breaking Energy,* July 31, http://bre akingenergy.com/2014/07/31/new-financing-options-for-coal-power-pla nts-through-the-brics-new-development-bank/

Rodrik, B. (1998). Why Do More Open Economies Have Bigger Governments? *Journal of Political Economy, 106*(5), 997–1032.

Romo, V. (2021). Pentagon Reverses Itself and Now Says a Deadly Kabul Drone Strike Was an Error. *NPR,* September 17, www.npr.org/2021/09/17/ 1038381206/drone-attack-afghanistan-civilians-pentagon

Slaughter, A. (2000). Building Global Democracy. *Chicago Journal of International Law, 1*(2), 10–17.

Strange, S. (1988). *States and Markets.* B. Blackwell, New York.

Strange, S. (1996). *The Retreat of the State: The Diffusion of Power in the World Economy.* Cambridge University Press, Cambridge.

van Evera, S. (1998). Offense, Defense, and the Causes of War. *International Security, 22*(4), 5–43.

Waltz, K. (1999). Globalization and Governance. *PS: Political Science & Politics, 32*(4), 693–700.

3 Politicism in Action

Post-Cold War Literature

The end of the Cold War brought a deluge of competing visions describing the future of the international order. Some ideas were hopeful that a new, peaceful, and democratic world underwritten by globalization was possible. Free trade would bring all states together under a global banner of peace and prosperity, especially for those that do not resist (neoliberal approach). Others saw this same force as destructive and exploitative (Marxist approach). Some saw this new world order dominated by the United States as temporary. Others advocated a proactive strategy for almost permanent unipolarity; competitor states must be kept at bay (neoconservative). There was also the worry that the United States would act unchecked as no great power could effectively balance against expansion, destabilizing the international system (realist). Other pessimists saw conflict between cultures (civilizational approach). The absence of the capitalist/communist ideological conflict would create new alliances and enemies.

This chapter emphasizes the utility of the Politicist analysis by illustrating the pseudoscientific nature of these works. Four main ideas dominated the Post-Cold War intellectual landscape. However, each proved to be flawed. For civilization or cultural conflict, Samuel Huntington's *Clash of Civilizations*, Benjamin Barber's *McWorld Vs. Jihad*, and Bernard Lewis' *Roots of Muslim Rage* will be discussed. The next to be addressed are the works of neoliberal scholars Francis Fukuyama's *End of History* and Friedman's *Lexus and the Olive Tree*. For Marxist literature, we will address Michael Hardt and Antonio Negri's *Empire* and Alex Callinicos' *Imperialism*. For neoconservativism, the work of Condoleezza Rice and Charles Krauthammer will be analyzed. These books were chosen because

DOI: 10.4324/9781003468677-3

they were definitive texts describing the Post-Cold War world. These samples made waves, highlighting the competing ideas of that period. These Politicist arguments focused more on a specific vision of the future, neglecting the possibility of state conflict or suggesting alternative units of governance (civilizations, democracy, human networks, etc.) as the solution to international conflict. Other works just stuck to a specific argument, like culture, extending it to all aspects of political life. These normative and unscientific processes must be identified as this is the first step of Politicist analysis. After summarizing these works, a short critique of each grouping will follow, testing the hypotheses with real-world data. This is the second step. The aim is to prepare for Chapter 4. Chapter 4 further tests the idea that no real change in international politics, or state behavior, can be expected without global systemic change. As identified in Chapter 2, power and state interests are central to international politics. Ignoring these factors will lead to incorrect conclusions about the processes of international politics.

Post-Cold War Literature: Culture Wars, Globalization, Empire, and State Power

Post-Cold War literature has four core themes: civilization, state power, globalization, and Empire. By grouping the literature into four categories, one might better be prepared to examine the foreign policy of the United States after the fall of the Soviet Union and other international developments. Politicist visions of the future world order were based on a pseudoscientific interpretation of trends and a specific vision of the future. These ideas shaped the policy and behavior of states within the global system. Misperceptions of the scientific method, specifically causal determinants such as what a "system" is, led to misunderstandings of the future.

Culture Wars

In *The Clash of Civilizations and the Remaking of World Order*, Huntington claims that "culture and cultural identities, which at the broadest level are civilizational identities, are shaping the patterns of cohesion, disintegration, and conflict in the Post-Cold War world" (1996, 20) that "societies sharing cultural affinities [will] cooperate" (ibid) and that "societies sharing cultural affinities cooperate" (ibid).

International behavior is a product of identities rather than states, their militaries, and interests in terms of survival. A form will ally itself with another state based on shared cultures and history rather than security concerns. Indeed, security concerns are driven by cultural and historical identities. Cooperation and conflict are thus determined by historical experience and cultural perspectives.

Huntington places no weight on states focusing solely on cultures and civilizations. There are nine civilizations: Western, Latin American, African, Islamic, Sinic, Hindu, Orthodox, Buddhist, and Japanese. States with common civilizational roots will band together under the leadership of one core state (ibid 238). For instance, Russia is the core state of Orthodox civilization. Orthodox states like Serbia, Belarus, and Ukraine will coalesce around Russia. Culture is thus the primary driver of politics as it provides specific ways of thinking and perceiving reality that supersedes materialism and political ideology (ibid 41). Huntington expected the world to seek a new way to organize beyond Cold War political struggles and (re)embrace cultural tradition and civilizational pride.

Huntington argues that the Cold War was a political, ideological struggle between capitalism and socialism. This ideological/political conflict surrounded materialist economic and political questions over the international system. The end of the Cold War signaled a new beginning, where people globally began to ask questions about their identity. Identities were lost or pushed aside during the Cold War. States had to choose between the United States and the Soviet Union. Both states were multi-ethnic, civic nationalist states. This political struggle determined international politics. The end of the Cold War brought a renewed effort to rediscover themselves and their broader civilization. This seemed genuine, especially since the end of the Cold War, the disintegration of the Soviet Union, and the birth of several newly independent states in the former Soviet political space. The collapse of Yugoslavia also shaped Huntington's perspective. He points to the increase in cultural/civilizational conflicts in 1993 as proof of his hypothesis: wars in the Caucuses and Yugoslavia and increases in Islamic terrorism and violence all pointed to a profound change in international politics. Cooperation between similar cultural states also pointed to this. For instance, the newly independent states in Eastern Europe were clamoring to join NATO. Huntington is thus arguing that the global order was much less a realist or liberal one determined by military or economic variables but rather an interpretive one driven by identities, ethnicities, religions, societies, tribes, histories, and cultural practices.

In retrospect, Huntington's formulation depends on emerging trends expanding to the entire globe. We can turn to his recommendations to further understand Huntington's Politicist perspective (ibid 311–312). Huntington saw the West as under attack from competitor civilizations, the most important of which were Islamic and Sinic (or Chinese) civilizations (ibid 312). To save Western civilization, Huntington advocates a proactive strategy of further integration between Western states within military, economic, political, and social realms. He also supports a sort of cultural imperialism of Latin America, recommending the "Westernization" of Latin America, encouraging this civilization to further align itself with the West. This theme is repeated in Japan and Russia. For instance, Japan must be enabled to align with the West, stopping its "drift" toward China. The West is to recognize Russian power as a core state within the Orthodox civilization, especially on its southern border. Huntington's final recommendation is most interesting: the West was "to recognize that Western intervention in the affairs of other civilizations is probably the single most dangerous source of instability and potential conflict in a multicivilizational world" (ibid 312). In many ways, Huntington's activism here seems to be to save Western culture from being swallowed up completely.

Huntington sees civilization conflict between the West and its partners on one side and Islamic and Sinic civilizations on the other as a possibility in the Post-Cold War world (ibid 312–313). Given the trends during this period, he is trying to understand the future. Unlike more optimistic scholars like the ones discussed in the next section, Huntington sees conflict on the horizon. Many scholars have ridiculed Samuel Huntington's *Clash of Civilizations* since his article in *Foreign Affairs*. People have called it racist and too simple, relying on gross oversimplification and Orientalism to argue (see Adib-Moghaddam 2014). After a careful reading, these criticisms seem exaggerated and sometimes inappropriate. First, Huntington says quite clearly that the West is not superior; civilizations are just different. He also goes on to say that civilizations may or may not have a core state, such as the Islamic and Latin American civilizations. Having read the book, this time with no preconceived notions, there are some successful predictions like the rise of China and Russia's reactions to NATO expansion. However, Huntington's perception of

Islamic civilization is the most difficult to understand within the historical context. Huntington admits that the Islamic civilization lacks a core state, divided by three potential leaders: Turkey, Saudi Arabia, and Iran. Yet, it is the Islamic grouping with the Sinic civilization that forms the greatest threat to the Western world. Further, given the rise of Islamic terrorism, one may assume that the Islamic civilization is fractious, and a united front seems improbable. However, Huntington was not alone. Other scholars, like Bernard Lewis, perceived the world similarly.

In 2002, Lewis Published *What Went Wrong? Western Impact and Middle East Response*, presenting the argument that Islamic civilization stagnated and remained in a perpetual decline after the European Renaissance period (Lewis 2002, 6). Since then, the Islamic culture has been in relative weakness, looking for something or some people to blame (ibid 152). The latter, "who," is central to Lewis' argument. Lewis argues that Muslims tend to blame groups of people for their civilization's decline: the Ottomans, the Mongols, European Imperialism and Colonialism, Zionists, and Americans are all to be blamed for their misfortune (ibid 159). Lewis argues that instead of attacking the West, the Muslim world should fight against Islamic terrorism by advocating for more freedom: "freedom of the mind from constraint and indoctrination, to question and inquire and speak' freedom of women from male oppression; liberty of citizens from tyranny—that underlies so many of the troubles of the Muslim world" (ibid 159). While seemingly noble, taking the diverse and divided Muslim world and directing them as one political unit is inherently incorrect.

Lewis' approach paints in broad brush strokes, generalizing the attitudes of Muslim peoples into one anti-Western platform. In response, he recommends that democracy and freedom abound. He neglects a variety of possible important variables and chooses to advance western norms. The Politicist framework identifies his clear bias toward the west, and this impacts his arguments. It is dangerous as such ideas are clearly represented in American foreign policy with the Bush administration's policy of bringing democracy to Iraq.

Like Lewis, Benjamin Barber argues similarly in his work. He looks much less at the civilization clash and more at the issue of capitalist encroachment on culture and civilization. The erosion of traditional life in the face of globalization may cause illicit violent rejections. McWorld versus Jihad struggles are the same side of the same undemocratic coin, where gaps in increased economic integration lead to a democratic deficit that cannot simply be remedied by capitalism. Islamic fundamentalism is driven by this desire to return to a more traditional society. This opposing force may result in terrorism. Like Lewis, Barber hopes that moderates from either camp seek out one another in hopes of finding a peaceful solution to the confrontation between civilizations. Such chaos will only destabilize the international order (Barber 1995).

Huntington, Lewis, and Barber agree on one major theme: that questions of culture remain central to the Post-Cold War world. Many see culture as of paramount importance to their lives and livelihood. However, during this particular junction, the forces of globalization seem to be just taking off. Globalization ultimately seems like a destabilizing force, as Huntington himself would remark that globalization pushes non-western peoples to preserve their culture as an integral part of their identity (Huntington 1996, 68). The global religious revival is one manifestation of this rejection of globalization. However, Huntington argues that it is not necessarily true that modernization due to globalization, somehow non-western peoples would lose their culture. He quotes Braudel by saying that it would be "childish" to think that globalization would necessarily end cultures instead of that non-western cultures would reshape the world through export. Non-western cultures would benefit from increased exposure which may even reduce the dominance of Western civilization. Said differently, globalization is not a "west versus rest" frontier. The world might become less Western and more "Western." However, some reject globalization fundamentally because of its Western bias (Barber 1995). These arguments, while interesting, neglect states and state power and, as we will see, do not stand up to the true nature of international politics.

American dominance of the international order after the Post-Cold War certainly had pessimists that regarded conflict, specifically civilizational conflict, as a real possibility. The culture was the basis for conflicts and cooperation within the international conflict. Since globalization was a product of American power and economic ideology (capitalism), people ultimately saw Americanism as the next possible step for the international order. Thomas Friedman and Francis Fukuyama are two scholars who actively advocated for this possibility. These two scholars adopt some semblance of the scientific method to generate their arguments. In Politicist fashion, they wanted a world order that subscribed to a specific vision. The first to be discussed here is Friedman.

Neoliberalism

Friedman's book *The Lexus and the Olive Tree: Understanding Globalization* argues that globalization is the future of global politics. The forces of globalization constrain state behavior, as a result, it is "not simply a trend or fad but is, rather, an international system" (1999, ix). If globalization is the new international system, the realist version is now defunct. The primary mover of international politics is not security but prosperity. It rewards good behavior and punishes evil. This means that the state is no longer critical, but global markets are. The forces of the free market then shape or cause states' behavior by giving it systemic qualities. Friedman defines what he means by the international system in this way. He argues that the Cold War system was a division in the bipolar balance of power (ibid 7). The global globalization system is characterized by integration and interdependence. Friedman defines globalization as

a dynamic, ongoing process ... the integration of markets, nation-states, and technologies to a degree never witnessed before—in a way that is enabling individuals, corporations and nation-states to reach around the world farther, faster, deeper, and cheaper than ever before, and, in a way that is enabling the world to reach into individuals, corporations and nation-states farther, faster, deeper, cheaper than ever before.

(ibid 9)

He then adds that there is a disciplining factor, that it "produces a powerful backlash from those brutalized or left behind by the new system" (ibid). Free market capitalism is the primary thrust behind globalization, and the more a state opens itself to this force, the more developed and wealthier that state becomes (ibid). Globalization has its own rules and norms that reinforce globalization as the new international system or the Golden Straitjacket.

Friedman defines the Golden Straitjacket: "as the defining political-economic garment of this globalization era" (ibid 104). This garment is dedicated to freeing up state constraints to international business-like deregulation, privatization, eliminating tariffs, and reducing

barriers to foreign investment (ibid 105). These policy changes nega-
tively impact state autonomy by opening up to international markets.
However, according to Friedman, such policy changes may benefit the
world as "no two countries that both have a McDonald's had fought a
war against each other since each got its McDonald's" (ibid 248). This
statement is not to be taken at face value, as the real crux is that states
who trade freely may not decide to go to war due to mutual interdependence (ibid 249). Friedman quotes Montesquieu and Norman
Angell to make these points. Combining these two ideas, Friedman
makes a straightforward argument that globalization creates specific
state behaviors. This makes globalization a systemic force. Since
systems produce particular behaviors, globalization provides the rules
of engagement.

Interestingly, at the very end of the book, Friedman argues that
globalization, even though it is the international system of the twenty-
first century, needs force or a stable power structure (ibid 464).
Globalization cannot be sustained by the free market alone but by
military power. He states that

> markets function and flourish only when property rights are secure
> and can be enforced, which, in turn, requires a political framework
> protected and backed by military power ... indeed, McDonald's
> cannot flourish without the McDonald Douglas, the designer of the
> US Airforce F-15 ... the hidden fist that keeps the world safe ... is
> called the US Army, Airforce, Navy, and Marine Corps ... paid for
> by American taxpayer dollars.
>
> (ibid)

American diplomacy is also essential (ibid). As a "geopolitical
shaper," the United States has a responsibility to protect this (or its)
system. Friedman is not just saying that globalization is the new international system; the United States' unipolar order is the international
system. Friedman's future looks bright if states and people adjust to
the latest global system. There is a degree of futurism in this work, that
if all things remain equal, the world will enjoy peace and prosperity.
This is pseudoscientific and Politicist as it assumes the absence of any
real state challenger; this counter-argument, as significant as it is, is
not confronted. Yet this postulation forms the lynchpin of Friedman's
argument, as he does not reasonably address state conflict. Francis
Fukuyama's work does the same.

In *The End of History and the Last Man*, he argues that liberal democracy is the victor of ideological conflict as no other competitor exists (2006, xi). He writes: "Liberal democracy may constitute the 'end point of mankind's ideological evolution' as the final form of human government" (Fukuyama 2006, xi). Since there are no ideological challengers to liberal democracy, the world has reached the pinnacle of social relations. Adopting the Hegelian approach suggests a historicist understanding of the world, as the present ultimately shapes the future. Minor movements like fascism, authoritarianism, and Islamic fundamentalism may continue to exist. Still, given the rapidly changing world (technology and economy), these forces will soon be forced to assimilate or be left in the dust.

Fukuyama also extends this argument to the realist notion of an anarchical international system. In the chapter "The Unreality of Realism" and "The Power of the Powerless," Fukuyama critiques realism as having flawed assumptions that may lead to incorrect analysis. He believes there is no real reason to believe that the state system or human nature naturally produces or promotes aggression, as described by Machiavelli and Hobbes (ibid 248; 254). Aggression and warfare may have other origins, such as imperialism or resources that might drive warfare. Fukuyama does not suggest that the new liberal world would suddenly transform human relations, that "liberal democracy constrains man's instincts for aggression and violence but that it has fundamentally transformed the instincts themselves and eliminated the motive for imperialism" (ibid 263). Fukuyama points to the absence of wars between democracies to prove that a peaceful world is possible. With no real competitor, liberal democracy has a real chance to blossom. Realist theories are thus less essential and possibly inappropriate for the new world order (283).

Like Friedman, Fukuyama suggests that this liberal democratic world order be backed up by military power. Unlike Friedman, who proposes the United States (and American taxpayers) should provide this function, Fukuyama recommends a pacifist union similar to the League of Nations:

> If one wanted to create a league of nations according to Kant's precepts, that did not suffer from the fatal flaws of earlier international organizations, it is clear that it would have to look much more like NATO than the United Nations, that is, a league of truly free states brought together by their common commitment

to liberal principles. Such a league should be more capable of forceful action to protect its collective security from threats from the non-democratic part of the world.

(282–283)

Military power would still be relevant, not to balance against competitor states but to protect and extend the liberal democratic order. Essentially, the *End of History* perpetuates itself, not simply by the force of ideas, economic productivity, or any other high moral value but through power, snuffing out any potential competitor to liberal democratic supremacy.

Of the work presented here, Friedman and Fukuyama are the worst Politicist offenders. The *End of History* argument shows a trajectory, an evolution of society, natural to the Hegelian dialectic. They see this progress as an improvement from previous international systems, and rightly so. However, this normative agenda ignores the essential nature of the international system as described by the realist approach. Other approaches, like Marxist approach, commit the same error.

Marxism and Postmodernism

Taken together, Friedman and Fukuyama provide a unique understanding of the world. They unapologetically advocate for their perspective, seeing it as morally valuable. Moving away from a system dominated by states and state competition is seen as good. The only wars would be against authoritarian states; rightly so; the more democracies out there, the more peaceful the world would be. These ideas were criticized as foolish by Marxists and other critical authors. Alex Callinicos refers to Friedman's proposition in *The World Is Flat* that globalization was "flattening and shrinking the world ... [creating a] much more diverse—non-Western, non-white—a group of individuals [and those individuals] are being empowered" (Friedman 2005, 12) as "boosterism," tied to the enthusiasm for the new world order rather than true scholarship (2009, 198). Callinicos goes further, referring to the same work as a "magnificently absurd potboiler" (ibid 6), nothing more than a way to make money by appealing to the masses.

Callinicos (2009) provides a more critical view of global politics. His book titled *Imperialism and Global Political Economy* describes the Post-Cold War world as one dominated by the United States. He quotes journalist Ron Suskin's conversation with an unnamed senior advisor to the George W. Bush administration: "We are an empire now, and when we act, we create our own reality" (quoted in Callinicos 2009, 1). Those remarks attest to the idea that the fall of the Soviet Union brought an end to any opposition to the American Empire. The United States was now free to export its will, interests, and political system internationally. American-styled imperialism involved

> the systemic economic and political domination of the global South by the rich countries of the North, a condition that bred what [Gunter] Frank called the "development of the underdevelopment" preventing any economic progress in the countries of the periphery.
>
> (ibid 5)

The New American Century would usher in one interpretation of international economics predicated on free trade, deregulation, and globalization. By reshaping the world's economic system, the United States would create an international superstructure reinforcing American power. Hence, Callinicos, Friedman, and Fukuyama's interpretation of the global order is not just wrongheaded but part of a broader imperialist strategy of the United States to dominate the international order. By defeating the economic world, the United States would be able to enact a political agenda that closely relates to its grand strategy of perpetual hegemony. He quotes several Marxist scholars from various periods, such as Fred Block, 1977 writes.

> Those who manage the state apparatus—regardless of their political ideology—depend on maintaining good economic activity. This is true for two reasons. First, the capacity of the state to finance itself through taxation or borrowing depends on the state of the economy. Second, public support for a regime will decline sharply if the regime presides over a drop in economic activity.
>
> (quoted in Callinicos 2009, 85)

By creating dependencies, the United States would be able to dominate the political behavior of states within the international system. This argument reflects the Dependency Theory and World Systems Approach, as lesser developed, peripheral states solely cater to the economic demands of wealthier, developed states. Hence, the United States is at the core of any international economic relationship. As the primary economic power, the United States can dominate the world's political system, making it a global empire. Unlike the past empires, power would be economic, not military.

Callinicos takes a Marxist approach but pinpoints the United States as the primary power source. He emphasizes the central importance of economic power and calls out its cheerleaders for what they are. Callinicos sees himself as part of the forces of resistance as he ends with some cheerleading of his own: "... I hope to have shown the kind of analytical purchase Marxist social theory still has in the twenty-first century" (ibid 227). He ends the book with a call to arms: "Knowing empire is part of fighting it" (ibid). So, like Fukuyama and Friedman, Callinicos is dedicated to his theoretical perspective. He sees himself as fighting the domination of capitalist ideas and seeking a more just global society (at least his interpretation as such). Hence, Callinicos is not simply describing the world; he is pursuing activism. This ideological commitment makes his work Politicist and normative rather than describing mechanisms driving international politics.

Callinicos is closer to a traditional Marxist explanation of global political economy. He refers to Postmodernism Marxist as "a virus" that is essentially boring and unconvincing (ibid 6). This is in response to the success of Michael Hardt and Antonio Negri's work *Empire,* published in 2000. Hardt and Negri combine Marxism with Postmodernism to bring forth a more nuanced view of global capitalism. For Hardt and Negri, the question was not who but where. The three authors agree that global capitalism is a force of imperialism (hence the term *Empire*). Whereas Callinicos' ontological focus was the power of the United States, Hardt and Negri saw power as an unseen force.

Empire was

> ... formed not based on the force itself but on the capacity to present force as being in the service of right and peace ... Empire is not born of its own will but rather called into being and constituted based on its capacity to resolve conflicts.
>
> (Hardt and Negri 2000, 15)

If a state or group of individuals practice ideas or behaviors not in line with established norms of capitalism or democracy, then that state or group would be punished. Thus, the power of ideas was at the center of politics. Punishing the unaligned would further eradicate bad actors to enlarge consensus (ibid). By constructing universal values, domestic actors worldwide would be held accountable by nondemocratic forces of the global order. Such work is postmodern as it borrows from Michel Foucault's concept of biopower. Biopower constructs how people live and behave. Biopower produces and reproduces life and, once that force is defined by global capitalism, reinforces a specific style of life and livelihood of people.

Foucault states, "The control of society over individuals is not conducted only through consciousness or ideology, but also in the body and with the body. For capitalist society, biopolitics is what is most important, the biological, the somatic, the corporeal" (Foucault quoted in ibid 27). Hardt and Negri go beyond a materialist/economic understanding of the global political economy and embrace an ideational, social superstructure, or subjective epistemology. Global capitalism is a disciplining force beyond states, the state system, or military power. Violating any norms of free market capitalism would bring violent reprisals from various sources. The empire is thus a force for "good" behavior based on consent and consensus; as the authors say, it is "not born of its own will but rather it is *called* into being and constituted based on its capacity to resolve conflicts" (ibid 15). Hardt and Negri's primary focus is the power of perceived universality of norms that establish behavioral expectations. If any actor were to step out of line, there would be a global adverse reaction that punishes that actor, not for the specific crime, but for defending the empire to protect the kingdom. This reinforces power and globalization against "the new barbarians and the rebellious slaves who threaten the order" (ibid 20).

Defining Empire as a normative force without a center is fundamental to Post-Cold War literature. Hardt and Negri study Fukuyama's *End of History* hypothesis and the idea that significant conflicts are over (ibid 189). Ideological struggles no longer exist: Empire exists without an "other" to challenge it. Minor conflicts like nationalist or Islamic fundamentalism may continue to exist, but as Fukuyama says, adherents can be neutralized. Like Friedman, any actor who dares defy the order's military power would destroy the Empire. More importantly, the Empire must continuously pursue threats of some form. Being under threat creates a sense of urgency that legitimizes drastic, violent action against the opponent. This requires constant expansion of the Empire's norms for its own sake. The aim is to encompass the entire globe. Hence, no alternative can be tolerated: the end of history is to be enforced. Under scrutiny, such a postulation does not hold water as state power, interests, and nationalism is still very relevant. We shall see this in the following section.

Neoconservativism

Hardt and Negri see a destructive future for the world. By defending the principles of the Empire, the Empire can be preserved for the foreseeable future. While Fukuyama and Friedman praise such a perceivable inevitability, Hardt, Negri, and Callinicos hope for change from a resistance network or multitude (ibid 60–66). Arundhati Roy (2004) focuses on what she thinks is at the center of global change: the United States. Unlike Hardt and Negri (like the other authors mentioned), the United States is the center of international political developments for the extension of its imperialist power. She writes that the United States is a "single empire with an arsenal of weapons that could obliterate the world in an afternoon hand as complete, unipolar, economic and military hegemony" (ibid 11). States that fit the mold, like Argentina at the time, would be heralded as beautiful examples of progress. Other states, like Iraq, would be punished for being the "black sheep" in the global political system. Other scholars praise this new world order. These authors see the world's future as inherently American, and military action must be taken to solidify American dominance and perpetuate it for centuries to come.

The *Foreign Affairs* article by Condoleezza Rice titled "Promoting the National Interest" (2000) is a significant representation of this confusion. She writes: "[the] the U.S. has found it exceedingly difficult to define its 'national interest' in the absence of Soviet power" (45). Rice may not be labeled a neoconservative, but her opinion embodies the ideology so well. In the article, Rice makes a compelling case for a new American-dominated system. She sees the unique moment gifted to the United States and argues that the United States is in a "remarkable position" (ibid 46). American foreign policy must thus advance American interests that would ultimately be in the best interests of world peace and prosperity (ibid 47). As ambiguous as this may sound, Rice does get specific in four bullet points:

- To ensure that America's military can deter war, project power, and fight in defense of its interests if deterrence fails;

- To promote economic growth and political openness by extending free trade and a stable international monetary system to all committed to these principles;
- To renew solid and intimate relationships with allies who share American values and can thus share the burden of promoting peace, prosperity, and freedom;
- To focus U.S. energies on comprehensive relationships with extensive powers, particularly Russia and China, and can and will mold the character of the international political system; and
- To deal decisively with the threat of rogue regimes and hostile powers, which is increasingly taking the forms of the potential for terrorism and the development of weapons of mass destruction (ibid 46–47).

Here, Rice is arguing for formulating an international system created and dominated by the United States for years to come. The third bullet point conveys this idea, while the others demonstrate how power (military, economic, and soft) is to be used to successfully "mold the character" of the international system.

The end of the Cold War also signaled a new beginning to the international order. This period is known quite ambiguously as the Post-Cold War. This was a confusing period as scholars and policymakers did not know the identification of the enemy other. After World War II, and even before that, many understood that the new enemy would be the Soviet Union. In many respects, Rice's article is similar to George Kennan's "X" article in the same outlet: *Foreign Affairs*. Kennan defines the problem (global Soviet competition) and outlines possible solutions, specifically containment and respecting prestige (Kennan 1947). Containment hopes to prevent any further expansion by the Soviet Union rather than forcefully and directly confronting it. Kennan expected the Soviet Union to collapse:

> But the possibility remains (and in the opinion of this writer, it is a strong one) that Soviet power, like the capitalist world of its conception, bears within it the seeds of its decay, and that the sprouting of these seeds is well advanced.
>
> (Kennan 1947)

The flaws in the Soviet political and economic system would eventually bring it down. Hence, Kennan's reasoning for containment. Rice sees the possibility of uninhibited American power and suggests shaping the international system for years to come. It is thus the responsibility of the United States to protect the global order: "If America wants stability, it will have to create it ... there will constantly be new threats disturbing our peace" (Rice 2000, 29).

Rice became a significant contributor to the Bush administration, and she certainly influenced its foreign policy. Other famous neoconservative writers advocate for the productive use of American military power. Charles Krauthammer was a significant figure. His article in *Foreign Affairs* titled *The Unipolar Moment* (1990) advocates for a direct, offensive, and impactful foreign policy to shape the structure of the international system for years to come. Krauthammer sees the United States as a force for good, not simply the purported good described by Hardt and Negri. For Krauthammer, overextension is not a real possibility, but if the United States were to collapse, it would be because of domestic economic disaster (ibid 26). Krauthammer sees these new threats as the proliferation of weapons of mass destruction and those states that seek such capabilities, like North Korea and Iraq (ibid 30). To describe these states, he coins the term "Weapon State" to highlight the authoritarian government's proclivity to destabilize the new liberal international system. Their drive to become a great power significantly threatens global stability. Krauthammer suggests that the United States develop robust strategies to protect the American unipolar moment, specifically denying potential competitors the technology needed for sophisticated weapons. He also goes beyond that:

> With the rise of the Weapons State, there is no alternative to confronting, deterring, and, if necessary, disarming states that brandish and use weapons of mass destruction. Moreover, there is no one to do that but the United States, backed by as many allies that will join the endeavor.
>
> (ibid 32)

Similar to Callinicos, he ends with a call to arms:

> We are in for abnormal times. Our best hope for safety in such times, as in difficult times past, is in American strength and will— the strength and will to lead a unipolar world, unashamedly laying down the rules of world order and being prepared to enforce them. Compared to the task of defeating fascism and communism,

averting chaos is a rather subtle call to greatness. It is not a task we are any more eager to undertake than the great twilight struggle just concluded. However, it is just as noble and just as necessary.

Krauthammer and Rice both see the American unipolar system as a productive force for security and stability, not just for the United States but the entire international system. They are eliminating threats to the international order before they will prolong unipolarity. In this way, power is used productively.

Obviously, neoconservative theorists are inherently Politicist. Like the Marxist discussed previously, there is an ideological, not a social scientific, used to understand international politics. The world is not a test tube used to conduct experiments. Such actions have consequences and may result in overextension and absolute decline leading to the rise of competitor states.

The Realist Critique

Of the literature discussed in this chapter, realism is less ideological and normative. Realists, specifically structural realists, see the world as anarchical (Waltz 2010). Waltz argues three types of international systems: unipolar, bipolar, and multipolar. These types are based on the number of great powers in the system (one, two, and more than two, respectively). For Waltz, the unipolar world might not be peaceful as the singular great power can act unchecked. This freedom may encourage the hegemonic state to overcommit its forces or lead to crusades to perpetuate power. This results in international political instability. Two authors make these predictions: John Mearsheimer's article *Why We Will Soon Miss the Cold War* (1990) and Kenneth Waltz's *Structural Realism after the Cold War* (2000) were two influential articles from two leading realist scholars in the International Relations subfield of International Security. They posit that the unipolar world would eventually return to a bipolar or multipolar competition in time.

Mearsheimer begins his article with a warning against the optimism defining the Post-Cold War period. He describes the Cold War era as tumultuous but ultimately easy to explain and predict state behavior (ibid 35). Those welcoming the new period as a peaceful and prosperous era may be wrong as they do not stand up to testing. Mearsheimer admits that many, including himself, do not quite understand the forces shaping the new world order. He expects increased state conflict, given that the bipolar balance of power has faded. Indeed, he has identified bipolarity as the source of peace for Europe since 1945. While neoliberals argue that prosperity would bring states together, using a period of peace and prosperity, Mearsheimer argues that such postulation is inherently wrongheaded. While it can be argued that individuals and businesses act in such a way, states do not. Individuals and companies may reside within legal structures. States do not. Taken together, states are motivated to survive as independent political units in an anarchical international system. States are concerned about relative gains, if one side may gain more than the other, then those gains will be used to dominate or annihilate them in the future. As a result, states do not trust trading partners. As Mearsheimer argues: "anarchy guarantees that security will often be scarce; this heightens states' concerns about relative gains, which makes cooperation difficult unless the pie can be finely sliced to reflect, and thus not disturb, the current balance of power" (ibid 45). Indeed, while optimists like Fukuyama and Friedman praise interdependence, Mearsheimer sees it as a source of eventual conflict as states seek to remain independent rather than become dependent on others.

Mearsheimer also believes that states tend to balance against threats. With the end of the Soviet Union, he expects the possibility of conflict within Europe itself. While he fully expected NATO to dissolve, given the absence of a threat, it simply did not occur. Instead, NATO membership increased, and their duties expanded into peace-keeping and peace-enforcing. However, he follows this with another significant point: while democracies may not fight against other democracies, they might undoubtedly start wars with nondemocracies or authoritarian regimes. Fukuyama, Friedman, Krauthammer, and Rice agree with this postulation, advocating for such aggressive foreign policy to secure American dominance.

Mearsheimer argues that the Soviet Union gave the free world an enemy to unite them. The end of the bipolar system may bring increased conflict among former European allies. He sees a resurgence of nationalism similar to Huntington but states that states and citizens can see beyond the chauvinism of the past. In all, he argues that the stability of the Cold War is gone, replaced by the unknown.

As a structural realist, Mearsheimer expects the international system to be in constant flux as power balances change. Waltz (2000) presents a structural argument that "changes of the system" may bring changes in state behavior, but "changes *in* the system would not" (ibid 5). This means that the world remains anarchic regardless of the victory of the United States and the spread of capitalism and democracy. States still engage in self-help behavior to survive, and power remains central to international politics (ibid). These three elements remain paramount as the global system has not changed. Instead, polarity has. While democracy and capitalism indeed have the opportunity to proliferate, the international system remains in place. Since the global system remains the main structural force that pushes states into war, war is still possible. As Waltz argues, "The structure of international politics is not transformed by changes internal to states, however widespread the changes may be. Without an external authority, a state cannot be sure that today's friend will not be tomorrow's enemy" (ibid 10). Waltz notices democracy's proclivity toward expansion and that state power left unchecked is prone to enlargement. He cites NATO expansion as a case in point. Interestingly, he discusses that NATO expansion might encourage the rise of authoritarianism in Russia as a rejection of Western encroachment (ibid 22). He expects that increased enlargement may push Russia to seek to balance against the United States as states seek security. However, the current conflict between the United States, the European Union, and Russia over Ukraine signals that power politics is still relevant. The Friedman neoliberal understanding that free trade will somehow make friends out of competitors and unify civilizations is ultimately wrong. The Realist position will be discussed further in Chapter 4, but for now it seems necessary to test the predictions discussed in this chapter.

Politicism in Action: Testing the Predictions—The Russia-Ukraine War (2022)

The Russia-Ukraine conflict marks a major test for international relations theories and perspectives, potentially challenging and possibly negating the Post-Cold War works discussed in this chapter. The Politicist nature of the authors created bad policies which led to global disorder, the rise of China, and the resurgence of Russia (Wang 2020; Sharafutdinova 2020). The point of contention for this chapter is that works that defined the Post-Cold War political environment discounted the state and state power due to historicist predictions based on pseudo-science. The first misunderstanding is the assumption that states, and power politics, would become less important or central due to the power of the free market. The Nord Stream pipeline is a clear case of interdependence (Borisov 2019). The development of the pipeline was an attempt to unite Russia with the European Union to facilitate better relations. The logic is that the more interdependence, the less likely the two countries would be driven to confrontation. Rather, they would seek other ways to solve their differences including further interdependence. If the European Union bought more natural gas, the European Union could move away from fossil fuels and nuclear power. This would result in a sum-sum outcome as the European Union would have better access to cleaner energy and Russia would have access to finance to assist development. This relationship benefitted both parties, and Russia has enjoyed increased wealth. More wealth led to increases in Russian military power. So, both Russia and the European Union met their goals; however, the problem is that Russia achieved traditional security goals while the European Union achieved nontraditional goals (environmental security, specifically a cleaner environment). Today, the European Union is dependent on Russian energy which ultimately reduces its political leverage against Russia. European states are dependent on Russia for gas, and this will influence their decision to confront Russian military action over Ukraine.

From this episode, it seems clear that Friedman and Fukuyama got it wrong. The world is still plagued by a conflict that cannot be considered a "one-off" by insignificant and weak actors. Russia is still a powerful state, and its behavior will define the competitive nature of the international system for many years to come. The free market does unite states into relationships of interdependence, but oftentimes that relationship is asymmetric (Keohane and Nye 1989). Asymmetric means that gains from engagement are not always evenly distributed (ibid). There is one power that will gain more, and those gains may work against the state as future leverage. Due to the dependence on Russia for gas, the European Union is at a disadvantage. Similarly, a drug addict and a drug pusher are locked in a relationship of interdependence, but ultimately one party, the addict, will not be gaining as much as the pusher, and the addict will have to submit to the whims of the pusher. The European Union will not have the financial clout to stop a Russian invasion. Further, the European Union is in an even more precarious situation than Russia as energy dependence dictates what it can and cannot do. President Putin has threatened to cut off supplies in the middle of winter in February (Catenacci 2022). This would be a humanitarian disaster with many people at risk of freezing to death.

Civilizational perspectives are also incorrect. Samuel Huntington specifically states that Ukraine and Russia will engage in friendly relations given their history as Eastern Orthodox states. He specifically applies his approach using the example of Russia and Ukraine, saying

> a civilization approach ... emphasizes the close cultural, personal, and historical links between Russia and Ukraine and the intermingling of Russians and Ukrainians in both countries, and focuses instead on the civilization fault lines that divide Orthodox eastern Ukraine from Uniate western Ukraine, a central historical fact of long standing which, in keeping with the "realist" concept of states as unified and self-identified entities Mearsheimer ignores.
>
> (Huntington 1996, 37)

This simply has not occurred. There has been constant tension between western-backed governments and Russian-backed governments as both wrestled for control of the entire country. However, Huntington is not saying that will be an absence of conflict. Conversely, he states that conflict will not be as bloody as contemporary conflicts during the time of writing:

> While a statist approach highlights the possibility of a Russian-Ukrainian war, a civilization approach minimizes that and instead highlights the possibility of Ukraine splitting in half, a separation which cultural factors would lead one to predict might be more violent than that of Czechoslovakia but far less bloody than that of Yugoslavia.
>
> (ibid)

We have the benefit of hindsight writing in February 2022 which is something that Huntington did not have. Unlike many of the authors critiqued in this article, we operate through retrodiction, studying events after they happen and looking for causal variables to explain and understand what happened. So, the ultimately incorrect prediction of Huntington, that his "... civilizational approach would encourage cooperation between Russia and Ukraine, urge Ukraine to give up its nuclear weapons, promote substantial economic assistance and other measures to help maintain Ukrainian unity and independence, and sponsor contingency planning for the possible breakup of Ukraine (ibid) is simply not occurring. The interesting thing is that before writing this, Huntington quotes Mearsheimer who says

> the situation between Ukraine and Russia is ripe for the outbreak of security competition between them. Great powers that share a long, unprotected border, like that between Russia and Ukraine, often lapse into competition driven by security fears. Russia and Ukraine might overcome this dynamic and learn to live together in harmony, but it would be unusual if they do.
>
> (Mearsheimer quoted in ibid)

Huntington sees Mearsheimer's policy as wrong because it would possibly legitimize Ukrainian nuclear capability; however, in many ways, this might have not been a bad thing as Ukraine would have to maintain deterrence in case of a Russian attack. Hence, the policy recommendations that might have helped Ukraine survive a Russian attack were more accurately predicted by Mearsheimer and his appreciation for power than Huntington's civilizational arguments.

Conversely, just because Huntington was wrong about Mearsheimer's position does not mean Mearsheimer is completely correct. Mearsheimer's position can be summarized by the simple idea that great power conflict may always be likely in an international system of anarchy. Russia will seek to undermine Ukrainian sovereignty and territorial integrity because NATO expansion is not in Russia's security interests. The same can be said about another conflict brewing but for different reasons: "if China continues its impressive economic growth over the next few decades, the United States and China are likely to engage in an intense security competition with considerable potential for war" (Mearsheimer 2006, 160). Mearsheimer argued this during a time of increased trade and investment between the United States and China, as other authors like Ikenberry (2002) and Freidman (1999) describe. It was thus not inevitable that China and the United States would just suddenly engage in conflict simply due to "impressive economic growth." In both cases today, Russia and China are indeed in conflict with the United States and the west. However, there might be other, more sophisticated, and complex ways that might better illustrate the competition dynamic we are now seeing. However, Mearsheimer's focus on power is essential to understand international politics, or any politics for that matter.

Hardt and Negri's power-centric analysis also comes close to reality. They criticize Fukuyama's *End of History* hypothesis as not an end of the conflict, but the beginning of an omni-crisis, meaning a large number of crises that will serve to reinforce the power of Empire (Hardt and Negri 2000, 189). Indeed, there have been several crises that have driven states closer together, all of which require an Other to unite against. First, it was terrorism. Terrorism dominated the international agenda until Donald Trump became president of the United States. Slowly but surely, he managed to securitize other issues like China and the "do-nothing Democrats." The Democratic Party, on the other hand, pursued a heavy anti-Russian line, arguing that Russia is the most important security threat and that Trump was a Putin puppet who actually "hacked" the election. Terrorism was pushed out of the way, and today the main emphasis is yet again Russia. Russian aggression against Ukraine has again united the "Empire" under one banner. The big Other is now Russia. Hardt and Negri put it simply "… Empire is formed not on the basis of force itself but on the basis of the capacity to present force as being in the service of right and peace" (2000, 15). Essentially then, rather than trying to solve the issue through negotiating, the world is united against Russia, with sanctions slowly destroying the Russian state and the potential prosperity of the Russian people.

Hardt and Negri are also locked up in their theory of choice. They see the world as structured by unseen forces of capitalism. There is no power center, and so states are no longer the driving unit of analysis for political outcomes. However, the actions of Russia, China, and the United States put these assumptions to the test. States still seem to be looking out for their interests in what seems to be an irrational way. In this regard, multiple centers of power are based on old ideas of nationalism, prestige, power, and interests. Hardt and Negri also got it wrong due to their ontological dedication to global markets. States still seem to be relevant actors.

Applying Mearsheimer's theory to the Ukraine-Russian conflict might seem correct on the surface. Indeed, there are two states at war, and NATO expansion was a major motivation for Russian action. However, if we were to look deeper, one might see other, more precise explanations. Some questions that go unanswered by Mearsheimer analysis are as follows:

1   Why would China, Russia, and the United States suddenly abandon mutually beneficial trade and exchange relationships?
2   Why would China, Russia, and the United States suddenly abandon international norms?
3   What role would authoritarianism play in relationship disruption?
4   What role did great power exceptionalism play in relationship disruption?
5   What intervening variables might be present to determine aggressive foreign policy, especially in the case of China?

It is rather interesting that only suddenly have Russia, China, and the United States started to risk a collapse of the international system over conflicts with likely negotiated settlements. Hardt and Negri's work creates a more sophisticated analysis, not just answering the *how* to question, but a *why* question, focusing on the wider framework of capitalism, division, legitimate violence, as well as definitions of "good" or "acceptable behavior" and "bad" or "unacceptable behavior." Mearsheimer might also be incorrect. Even though he did see the likelihood of conflict between Russia and Ukraine, he did emphasize the importance of Ukraine being a buffer state (Mearsheimer 2014). Mearsheimer did not realize that Ukraine could very well be irrational, seeking closer relations with the west even though such action threatened Russia. States do not seem to be rational or unitary. As such, the foreign policy of a nation might be a mishmash of various interests competing for dominance. This might explain the illogical and sporadic foreign policies of democracies with no real priority: willing to do everything but nothing well. Realism in this context is unrealistic in the sense that it cannot explain or predict. It relies on a normative framework that is inherently incorrect as it does not explain how states behave but rather how states should behave.

Is the current conflict over Ukraine an anomaly or it is an integral part of the international order and power politics? This major confrontation is a defining moment for the multipolar world. If Russia continues its war against Ukraine, it will show that national security still matters, that power politics is still the defining factor in international relations, and that other matters like civilizations, free trade and interdependence, and the international regime are secondary. Regardless of western sanctions, the violation of international norms, trade agreements, and so on, Russia seems determined to pursue its aims in Ukraine. This decision was not made in a vacuum; they were made considering the first confrontation over Crimea following increased western interests in Ukraine, a fact that threatened Russia. The question is: why? American dominance is thus a threat to Russia and possibly other powers in the international system. Waltz states that China "will emerge as a great power without trying very hard so long as it remains politically united and competent" (ibid 32). Writing in 2000, Waltz fully expects the rise of China and Russia as they seek to balance against the United States. The fact is that liberalism has yet to be translated as a framework for interstate intercourse accounting for political accountability and complete transparency. However, regardless of transparency and accountability infrastructures being factored in, one can never be sure of the intentions of others. Weapons used for defensive purposes to protect interests might also be perceived as aggressive. China might start overturning the system justifying its action defensively, as we are seeing with the prospective take-over of Taiwan sold as simply part of its territorial integrity. For Waltz, the enthusiasm expressed for the unipolar order is altogether incorrect as the competitive international system continues to exist. The unipolar order would be temporary as Russia and China would rise to balance against it. China, Russia, and other states, threatened by this unipolar order, would seek to check the unbridled power of the United States to preserve their survival as independent political units.

Conclusions: Summarizing the Four Schools of Thought

The four scholars here—neoliberals, Marxists, neoconservatives, and realists—perceive changes in the international political order after the fall of the Soviet Union. Neoliberals are neoconservatives who embrace change, hoping for perpetual American supremacy. Marxists are more critical, seeing the possibilities for global destruction and instability. Which vision is closer to the truth? Which theory describes international politics best? The following section evaluates these ideas relating to the past twenty years to illustrate the power of Politicist analysis, specifically scholar ideological commitment.

At every crucial moment and critical juncture in international relations, scholars describe the world and then prescribe measures for states to take. The literature discussed above differs widely from the events that unfolded after the Cold War. Of course, there were moments when scholars were correct. Huntington might have explained and rightly predicted ethnic violence in Yugoslavia, between Russia and Chechnya, the Rwandan genocide, the attacks on September 11, and other civilization conflicts between Russia and the West over Ukraine. The European Union as a supranational bloc is another fine example of civilizational coalescence. Fukuyama, Friedman, Hardt, Negri, and other Marxists discussed here are also correct as capitalism has an attached disciplinary aspect. Those states that do not fit into the capitalist-democratic frame are cast aside as pariahs or rogue states. Those states that work is rewarded by increased trading ties and ranking indices like the Freedom Index or the East of Doing Business Index. The indices encourage businesses and investors to do business in these particular states, leaving the lesser developed states with socialist/communist/religious governments, serious terrorist or organized criminal groups, and systemic corruption isolated from the global political economy.

Even though these authors got some things correct, major flaws are found in their arguments to ideological dedication. Significant changes in the international system, that is, the rise in challenger states (China and Russia), were largely ignored. Liberals believed that one liberal system would be created that would last seemingly forever. While such a world would inevitably be boring, it would be without conflict. This is the *End of History* hypothesis and Friedman's understanding of the American power project. Marxists pushed aside excellent power conflict, focusing on the global economy's power. Civilizational theorists might have predicted conflict between civilizations, but not across states and the state system. While it is correct that the Chinese and Russian systems are now in battle, this was not the case before 2014 in the case of Russia and in 2016 with the election of Donald Trump and his nationalist political and economic platform. The other important issue is that Russia and China had designs for a multipolar international system. In other words, Russia and China planned to increase their power in the United States and reduce it. In a global systemic sense, the most critical issue is relative power, not absolute power. China and Russia cooperated because they served to gain perceivably more than the United States. The United States was not in relative strength but in absolute power (Grieco 1988). Now that the world is changing, the United States is seeking to correct the power imbalance while maintaining constructive relations with China. China is also seeking to amend the status quo international order by threatening to invade Taiwan.

Further, China is using its economic power to develop dependencies on weaker, more fragile developing states in Africa and the South Pacific (Solomon Islands). Australia has felt this brunt as its asymmetrically interdependent relationship with China has gone sour over Australia's membership in the Quadrilateral Alliance, or the Pacific NATO. The same goes for Russia and the European Union. Russia and the European Union cooperated well until Russia perceived its near-abroad (Ukraine) as moving too close to the West. The annexation of Crimea and the full-scale invasion of Ukraine in 2022 marked a significant departure. Russia sacrificed its mutually beneficial relationship with the European Union to invade Ukraine. However, due to European dependence on Russian oil and gas, Russia wields serious leverage on the continent. These issues will be expanded on in the following chapters, but they are worth mentioning here.

The international system is in the transition process, but this has been in the making since the end of the Cold War. The issue is that China and Russia have different interests than the United States. The United States acts to defend the status quo by acting, in many ways, as a world policeman. For instance, when Iraq invaded Kuwait, the United States rallied the international system to restore the status quo order. Iraq sought forced unification with Kuwait, given the Iraqi position that Kuwait was always part of Iraq. China and Russia have very different designs from their history and perceived status in the international system. Like Iraq, China and Russia seek to adjust the status quo to what they perceive as just, suiting their interests and prestige as great powers: China will seek to annex Taiwan and ethnically Russian-populated parts of Ukraine. The United States has as much to blame for this instability due to several foreign policy and domestic blunders that led to its decline. These foreign policy mistakes were not created in a vacuum but are related to the literature discussed by significant authors like Fukuyama and Friedman, underscored by exceptional ideals of the United States, like liberal democracy and free market capitalism.

The 1990s had a few episodes of interventionist foreign policy for the United States, such as the first Iraq War and Somalia. Nothing was to compare with what was to take place after the terror attacks of September 11. The United States embarked on two wars: Afghanistan and Iraq. At the same time, Candidate George W. Bush campaigned on notions of traditional Realism and principles of Self-Help (it was not the duty of the United States to act as the world's policeman). All this was to change. For the United States to be safe, it had to go on the offensive. This strategy became known as the Bush Doctrine. Rogue states were called out and labeled the Axis of Evil: Iraq, Iran, and North Korea. The world would be more secure by creating democracies where there were none. The United States had to finance this change because it was the world's only superpower (Jervis 2005). Since Fukuyama argues that there are no significant ideological competitors to American-style capitalism and democracy, these ideologies represent the pinnacle of human progress and will define progress in the future. As the end of progress and the final form of human government, all states would eventually adopt democracy and free market capitalism. For example, President Bill Clinton expressed the hope that one day China would soon become a democracy through the development of robust trade networks:

> Today the House of Representatives has taken a historic step toward continued prosperity in America, reform in China, and peace in the world. If the Senate votes, as the House has just done, to extend permanent normal trade relations with China, it will open new doors of trade for America and new hope for change in China … We will be exporting, however, more than our products. By this agreement, we will also ship more of our most cherished value, economic freedom.
>
> Bringing China into the WTO and normalizing trade will strengthen those who fight for the environment, labor standards, human rights, and the rule of law.
>
> For China, this agreement will increase the benefits of cooperation and the costs of confrontation.
>
> America, of course, will continue to defend our interests. Still, at this stage in China's development, we will have a more positive influence with an outstretched hand than a clenched fist … Though China may change, we all know it remains a one-party state that denies people the right to free speech and religious expression. We know that trade alone will not bring freedom to China or peace to the world.
>
> That is why permanent normal trade relations must also signal our commitment to permanent change. America will keep pressing to protect our security and advance our values. The vote today is a significant boost to both efforts, for the more China liberalizes

its economy, the more it will liberate the potential of its people to work without restraint and to live without fear

(Clinton 2000, *Associated Press*)

So dominant were Fukuyama and Friedman's ideas that their neo-liberal ideas made it to the White House. The "high" or "euphoria" of the Cold War's end shaped the American leadership's minds. The Marxist critique correctly described this new world. However, it also ignored state competition seeing the globalized world as the new normal.

One issue liberal and Marxist authors agreed on is that any group or state outside the liberal democratic order would be disciplined. For instance, Friedman and Fukuyama both argued that there might always be nationalist or religious violence that prefers a more traditional way of life. However, these groups will either assimilate over time or die off, as Fukuyama assumes people naturally yearn for freedom. This is the Marxist theoretical expectation. By 2002, many argued that Iraq and others needed little help to become free (Jervis 2005, 80). Any state or person criticizing these efforts was considered an enemy as you were either "with us or against us" mentality dominated the global political landscape (Bush quoted in CNN November 6, 2001). Force was being used to perpetuate American hegemony, yet this mission led to overextension and significant losses in American reputation, power, and status. Overextension would, in time, lead to systemic change.

Realists highlighted the eventual transformation of the international system from unipolar to multipolar. During the 1990s, the United States expanded its influence across the world. No other state could challenge the United States during this period. China moved closer to the United States economically, intertwining its economy deep into the United States. This relationship of complex interdependence was vital to China's continuing economic success. This process of globalization continued and increased throughout the decade until Barack Obama's steel tariffs declined further with the election of Donald Trump. The disruption of Donald Trump seems to be a sort of realist answer to the international political environment. However, he has reshaped the perception of the international arena and, in many ways, brought about severe changes in American foreign policy.

Chapter 4 dives deeper into structural realism, explaining what a "system" means as a driving force of state behavior. It will then illustrate the history of globalization as a history of state power. Globalization was supposed to bring states together under American hegemony, yet it gave rise to China and Russia. This will help better understand the dangers of normative designs within scholarship. The final section illustrates that multipolarity was China's and Russia's aim. In retrospect, the signs between China and Russia are clear that both rising powers would seek to balance against the United States. Given their history and prestige, it was natural to expect the rise. However, enthusiasm for the American-led new world order could have distracted scholars from this potential outcome. Politicist analysis holds these ideas accountable by highlighting the pseudoscientific nature of Post-Cold War theories and ideas shaping American foreign policy.

References

Adib-Moghaddam, A. and Oxford University Press. (2014). *A Metahistory of the Clash of Civilizations: Us and Them Beyond Orientalism*. Oxford University Press, Oxford.

Barber, B. (1995). *Jihad vs. McWorld*, 1st ed, Times Books, New York.

Borisov, A. Y. (2019). International Business and the Crisis of Globalization. *Vestnik MGIMO-Universiteta, 3*(66), 61–88.Callinicos, A. (2009). *Imperialism and the Global Political Economy*, Polity Press, Cambridge.

Catenacci, T. (2022). *Conservative Daily News: Russia Cuts Off Key Gas Pipeline to Europe amid Rising Tensions*. Newstex, Riviera Beach, Florida.

Clinton, B. (2000). President Clinton's Remarks on the Passage of the China Trade Bill. *The Associated Press*, May 25 https://archive.nytimes.com/www.nytimes.com/library/world/asia/052500clinton-trade-text.html.

CNN. (2001). You Are either with Us or against Us. *CNN*, November 6, 2001, accessed April 11, 2023 https://edition.cnn.com/2001/US/11/06/gen.attack.on.terror/.

Friedman, T. (1999). *The Lexus and the Olive Tree*. Farrar, Straus, Giroux, New York.

Friedman, T. (2005). *The World Is Flat: A Brief History of the Twenty-first Century,* Farrar, Straus and Giroux, New York.

Fukuyama, F. (2006). *The End of History and the Last Man*. Free Press, New York.

Grieco, Joseph M. (1988). Anarchy and the Limits of Cooperation: A Realist Critique of the Newest Liberal Institutionalism. *International Organization, 42*(3), 485–507.

Hardt, M. and Negri, A. (2000). *Empire*, Harvard University Press, Cambridge.

Huntington, S. (1996). *The Clash of Civilizations and the Remaking of the World Order*, Simon and Schuster, London.

Ikenberry, G. J. (2002). *America Unrivaled: The Future of the Balance of Power*, Cornell University Press, Cornell.

Jervis, R. (2005). *American Foreign Policy in a New Error*, Taylor & Francis, New York.

Kennan, G. (1947), The Sources of Soviet Conflict. *Foreign Affairs,* www.for eignaffairs.com/articles/23331/x/the-sources-of-soviet-conduct.

Keohane, R and Nye, J. (1989). *Power and Interdependence*, Harper Collins, New York.

Krauthammer, C. (1990). The Unipolar Moment. *Foreign Affairs*, *70*(1), 23–33.

Lewis, B. (2002). *What Went Wrong: Western Impact and Middle Eastern Response*, Oxford University Press, Oxford.Mearsheimer, J. (1990). Why We Will Soon Miss the Cold War. *The Atlantic Monthly (1993)*, *266*(2), 35–7,40.

Mearsheimer, J. (2006). China's Unpeaceful Rise. *Current History*, *105*(690), 160–162.

Mearsheimer, J. J. (2014). Why the Ukraine Crisis Is the West's Fault. *Foreign Affairs* *93*(5). www.foreignaffairs.com/articles/russia-fsu/2014-08-18/ why-ukraine-crisis-west-s-fault

Rice, C. (2000). Promoting the National Interest. *Foreign Affairs*, www.for eignaffairs.com/articles/55630/condoleezza-rice/campaign-2000-promot ing-the-national-interest.

Roy, A. (2004). The New American Century. *The Nation,* January www.thenat ion.com/article/archive/new-american-century/.

Sharafutdinova, G. (2020). *The Red Mirror: Putin's Leadership and Russia's Insecure Identity*. Oxford University Press, Oxford.

Waltz, K. (2000). Structural Realism after the Cold War. *International Security*, *48*(2), 5–41.

Waltz, K. (2010). *Theory of International Politics*, Addison-Wesley, Reading, MA.

Wang, Y. (2020). 'The Backward Will Be Beaten': Historical Lesson, Security, and Nationalism in China. *The Journal of Contemporary China*, *29*(126), 887–900.

4 Politicism in Action II
What Happened?

Chapter 3 discusses significant intellectual developments after the Cold War and discusses the ideological commitments expressed as part of the Politicist analysis methodology. Speculating on the future of world politics is natural during times of uncertainty. Each author interpreted the world differently based on their deeply established beliefs about the international order. A Marxist interprets events in a much different way than a liberal. When the Soviet Union was established, it was expected that a Marxist would envision a better world while a liberal may mourn the loss. This process is straightforward, showing American unipolarity after the Cold War. What is less obvious is the civilizational arguments. Why did Huntington, Lewis, and others see the world as broken up into civilizations, with the Islamic culture being seen as the greatest threat to Western liberal democracy? It is possible that these authors' expectations could be related to events.

A Western victory was also a victory for the culture of the West and its political system. Religious and ethnic tensions were rising and could be interpreted as a civilizational reaction to Western cultural imperialism. Marxist scholars would agree, as global capitalism had no real opponent. Hardt and Negri's work understood this danger well. As described in the introduction, state power seemed to decline, and the ontological unit was a global capitalist class free of national or state constraints. However, as realists did, it is essential to note that while state autonomy seemed in decline, the international system was still anarchic. The United States was the most potent state but could not control global political outcomes for long. Terrorism, organized crime, climate change, economic instability, human security, and the

DOI: 10.4324/9781003468677-4

state system's status quo were too much for one state and its taxpayers to handle. Of course, liberal thinkers were not as skeptical or pessimistic. For these authors, progress would only go up as the United States now had the power to recreate the world in its image. This exceptionalism would be a significant driving force for American foreign policy, precisely its neoliberal free trade form in the presidencies of Bill Clinton and Barack Obama or its neoconservative form in George W. Bush. Neoliberal free trade policies led to the rise of China, as jobs and investments brought wealth and power to China and Russia (European Union oil and gas dependence). Neoconservative policies led to failed American democracy projects in Afghanistan and Iraq. Hence, by giving wealth to China and Russia and losing wealth in Afghanistan and Iraq, the United States lost its unipolar moment.

In an effort to illustrate the mechanics of Politicist analysis, this chapter will preview the events of the past thirty years to understand whether or not the trends lined up with scholar expectations. For most of the explored works, it is essential to note that the attacks on 9/11 had not happened. However, even if 9/11 did not occur, it is likely that if left unchecked, the United States would waste its unipolar moment, and other powers would inevitably rise. The international system could have shifted to multipolarity, given the American hegemony's threat to Russia and China. Krauthammer fully expected that the United States' "unipolar moment" would end if there was an economic calamity. The 2008 financial crisis was a catastrophe, and the United States experienced an absolute decline following the economic shock. Few scholars, except maybe Huntington and Lewis, expected or predicted the attacks on 9/11. The 9/11 attack led to the misadventures in Afghanistan and Iraq, which, coupled with the 2008 financial crisis, led to multipolarity: China's rise, Russia's resurgence, and the BRICS collaboration.

This chapter seeks to underscore the importance of the structure of anarchy and the state system to understand the nature of international politics. Since realism does not have any real normative commitment, it may have been better prepared to predict the evolution of the international system. The international system is not based on cultures or democratic norms, but on self-help, as great powers shape the political behavior of one another. Any world hegemon is doomed to be short-lived, as rival states will rise to balance against it. The following section describes the evolving nature of global trade and cooperation since the nineteenth century. Specific attention to the monetary competition today will underscore the central importance of power and competition over globalization. The final part of the chapter describes the attempts by Russia and China to balance against the United States. The Primacov Doctrine and China's development strategy are two manifestations of competitor multipolar drive. China and Russia were threatened by the unipolar system of the United States and were driven to balance against it. This motivation shaped their foreign policy behavior and created a multipolar world. Unipolarity was thus a significant threat to Russia and China. By rebalancing the international order, these states could feel more secure in the face of American dominance. By focusing on power and interests rather than normative commitments, realist prediction seems to have bested the rest. Within the Politicist analysis methodology then, and the benefit of hindsight, this is safe to say. Interestingly, the same might be said for Marxist analysis.

The final part of this chapter discusses the evolution of political ideology by considering ongoing challenges to liberal democracy, especially in the United States. Today, elections are called into question: Hillary Clinton questioned the results of the 2016 election blaming Russia for interfering in the election. In 2020, Donald Trump launched accusations of cheating and fraud. Looking back, the *End of History* may not even hold for the United States. As inequality and economic uncertainty increase, people will question the sustainability of capitalism and liberal democracy. This is not to sound the alarm or to argue that the world is headed toward authoritarianism, but to say that the potential is always there. Liberal democracy and capitalism are not automatic, nor do they work all the time properly. There is always a need to improve and encourage the resilience of these political-economic systems. Marxist critiques remain credible: an expansionary form of capitalism is socially and environmentally destructive. Checks and balances on these systems to ensure their sustainability, in the long run, is an ever-present effort.

Politicist Testing: Power Transition and the Continued Relevance of the State in Anarchy

Power is the ultimate arbiter of international politics, and any vision of the international order must incorporate power into its analysis. The thesis of this chapter is that the structure of the international system, anarchy, results in state competition. This means that a multipolar system would eventually replace any unipolar order. In Chapter 3, we discussed the literature of the 1990s unified by one sole idea: that state competition would soon be replaced by something else (whether global capitalism or civilizational clash). This section shows that anarchy and state competition are ever-present in world politics. Any attempt at the exchange between states resulted from state interests; powerful states formulate the infrastructure around which states cooperate. If states deem it necessary to change the cooperative system into a competitive one, the system would again change. This seems most evident by summarizing the last two hundred years of globalization. This idea will be tested by conducting a historical analysis, beginning with the British and ending with the current system. Studying history reveals repeated patterns of behavior. These patterns should be given weight over ideological commitments as part of Politicist analysis.

Before World War I, the world was managed under an automatic system of monetary governance. Monetary systems are needed to facilitate trade by creating rules and norms that actors follow (Keohane 1984; Krasner 1983). These rules develop expectations required for states to have the confidence to trade. The Classical Gold System emerged during the 1870s and was first unilaterally adopted by Great Britain, the world's dominant power and financial center. Other countries quickly followed the world's economic hegemon. The more people joined this system, the more advantages gained, and the more trade flourished. The main benefit was the ability to trade internationally and exchange rate stability. Economists understand this as "network externalities," that is, the more nations followed suit, the more benefits were gained (Bothwell et al. 2016; Oatley 2010, 220). In this system, all currencies were fixed to gold. This made nations economically secure relative to one another. Countries traded with each other and recorded the inflows and outflows in the balance of payments account (ibid). The balance of payments account records transactions between a nation and the rest of the world. This account was made up of two fundamental features: the current version, which records the trade of goods and services, and the capital account, which records financial transactions like the net national ownership of assets, such as foreign direct investment and purchases of stocks and government bonds (Higgins and Klitgaard 2007, 1).

The Gold Standard system brought significant increases in wealth, and states followed the rules of this regime due to gains (Bothwell et al. 2016). Cooperation helped define state expectations and gave one another the confidence to trade. During this period, we see an unprecedented rise in international trade and cross-border financial flows (ibid). However, even after many years of work and exchange, state competition destroyed the confidence to trade. World War I saw the world's most significant powers go to war, ultimately sacrificing global trade and cooperation under the Gold Standard.

At the beginning of the twentieth century, Britain's economy might became increasingly challenged by other nations like the United States and the German Empire. When World War I finally broke out in 1914, the European countries, led by Great Britain and France, borrowed heavily from the United States, which followed a stringent isolation policy. By the war's end, the United States emerged as the world's most potent power, both economically and politically. It held most of the world's debt and refused to forgive them (ibid). No power was willing and able to reorganize the world economically. Britain was no longer the most powerful nation and, thus, could not lead the new world economic order. The United States embraced a policy of isolation (ibid). Therefore, states were left without an international monetary regime. During these tumultuous and uncertain times, countries abandoned the Classical Gold Standard system and followed a floating exchange policy. This was due to the existence of war debt, German reparations, and the failure to settle these contentious and provocative issues. This led to a further reluctance to form a steady international monetary regime as nations previously did (ibid). The United States' institutionalization of the Smoot and Hawley Tariff of 1930 (due to domestic economic problems) led to further isolation. The ensuing wild fluctuations of the nation's exchange rate led to the establishment of the Reciprocal Trade Agreements Act of 1934 between the United States and twenty-seven countries. This led to some stability, but it was not enough to create a fully open international economic structure (ibid). The world, during this time, broke into several regional trading blocs of the liberal democratic, communist, and fascist kinds. There was no comprehensive monetary regime to define the nation's expectations. These sorts of divisions and uncertainties defined this era and led (along with other factors) to World War II.

After World War II, it became apparent that the United States had to emerge from its isolation to take on a more active role in achieving world economic stability and political security. New threats could only be curbed through cooperative military and financial means. The United States assumed a significant effort to construct a system that would ensure stability and define expectations through a regime. This was done to recreate the prosperity of the nineteenth century. Led by the intellectual prowess of Harry Dexter White and John Maynard Keynes, the United States and Great Britain published the "Joint Statement" that called for establishing an international monetary regime that took the form of solid, international economic institutions. Thus, the Bretton Woods system came into being to guarantee a stable exchange rate to promote international trade. The US government pegged its currency gold at $35 an ounce, and other states pegged their currencies to the USD (Gilpin 2001, 236). Governments had a duty to maintain that price. However, if countries faced a fundamental disequilibrium, they were allowed to change the exchange rate. Intellectuals and policymakers understood the dangers these two exchange rates (a stringently fixed or an excessively floating rate) had on cooperation: a middle ground had to be established. It was done through the Bretton Woods monetary regime (Gilpin 2001, 235).

The Bretton Woods system incorporated much of the Gold Standard System into its design. Governments were not allowed to adjust their monetary policy to spur growth. They were only permitted to lower their interest rate to maintain the exchange rate system. However, there were occasions when countries disobeyed the rules due to domestic economic pressure (Bordo 2020). There was indeed a desire to perfect this very rigid monetary system.

In the Post-War period, the United States reins the Western world order as the hegemon. European powers were exhausted after the war. The United States financed the European recovery through the Marshal Plan, which led to balance of payments deficits (Holm 2017, 118). As USD flowed from the United States into Europe, the Europeans used them to pay for imports from the United States and other countries. This led to balance of payments deficits which only worsened with the Vietnam War and the domestic welfare programs. The US government refused to raise taxes which reduced the USD value. States seeing the reduction in the value of the USD demanded goals in return so much that the United States could not meet these demands. This dollar overhang placed enormous pressure on the viability of the Bretton Woods system (Viksnins 1973). The United States refused to correct these structural weaknesses, such as reducing spending and increasing taxes, as there were real fears of a global recession. Eventually, the United States simply canceled the Bretton Woods system by floating the currency rather than continuing pegging it to gold. Confidence in the dollar further eroded, and this led to speculative attacks. Strange discusses this in her book *Casino Capitalism* (Strange 1988). The dollar was primed for devaluation, and actors were ready to pounce and make money from it, regardless of the consequences. This, along with nations' demand for gold, was the last straw. Nixon suspended dollars for gold and enacted a 10 percent surcharge on imports (Oatley 2010, 232). Other nations, like Germany, could no longer support the system and began to float their currency. Finally, governments attempted currency realignment at the Smithsonian, initially succeeding but failing. All in all, with the increases in the price of oil and other exogenous economic crises, nations began to float their currencies.

Bretton Woods was established to assist in exchange rate difficulties and enable international trade. This monetary regime made it easier for countries to adjust their policies without upsetting the global exchange rate system. However, the Bretton Woods system soon collapsed into a floating exchange regime due to several political and economic issues. Nations now follow a Non-System, as Robert Gilpin argues (Gilpin 2001). Some, like the United States, follow a floating exchange system determined by the financial markets. Others, like the European Union, pursue a fixed exchange system.

Consequently, how has the lack of a world system and the diversified and divided exchange rate systems among nations and blocs impacted international cooperation? Unlike the Bretton Woods system, world cooperation within this Non-System is informal and erratic. Often, there are calls for increased collaboration. In the 1980s, nations cooperated. The best example was the Plaza Accord when the Group of 5 (G5) came together to reduce the dollar's value (Bergsten and Green 2016). Their actions, which included German and Japanese currency appreciation, achieved the goal, and the dollar was devalued by 40 percent. Since the 1980s, however, there has been a stark lack of cooperation (ibid). Due to the growing size of international markets, such collaboration has been deemed too costly and, sometimes, futile. Thus, within this Non-System regime, expectations are not clearly defined, adversely affecting cooperation.

Cooperation facilitated through hegemons or international monetary regimes (formed by central states) is needed to correct economic crises. Collaboration among nations should never be taken for granted. For example, immediately following the financial crisis of 2008, little to no cooperation, except among the G7, was produced. Other nations from Europe, Latin America, and the East Asian powerhouses offered no moral suasion. Where was cooperation when it counted? Why aren't states cooperating more vigorously "After Hegemony"? It is in the interest of those nations who have gone silent to act. China, for example, trades mainly with the Western world. If the American economy collapses, they will do the same. All actors have something to lose if the United States falters. Therefore, cooperation is needed to create a new financial system based on efficiency and stability. Currently, and we cannot expect this in the long term, we do see cooperation and understanding between these two economies. Asian central banks are incurring losses to support the dollar, something we did not see with Germany before the fall of the Bretton Woods system. Simultaneously, US monetary authorities maintain low short-term interest rates to encourage Asian purchases of US securities. In this way, Asian economies are shoring up the USD value to sustain their capacity and strength to trade (Quiggin 2004, 3). This is inherently the culture of cooperation that must continue within the international trade and monetary regime so states may continue trading.

Today's international economic system is different from previous periods. The Non-System continues to exist, but state conflict and economic instability present a serious challenge today. The United States has dominated world financial markets as well as the world's financial infrastructure (e.g., the Society for Worldwide Interbank Financial Telecommunications [SWIFT] system since the end of the Cold War (Cesarano 2006; Holm 2017; Boughton 2001)). The United States is leveraging its position to punish states for any act deemed outside established normative behavior. The United States is now punishing Russia for its invasion of Ukraine by banning it from SWIFT. The United States is also freezing Russian assets in Western banks to destroy the Russian economy (U.S. Department of the Treasury 2022). However, in response, Russia is demanding payment in rubles even though existing contracts state that the price is in USD (D'Emilio and Moulson 2022). This strategy increased the demand for rubles as states in need of Russian oil, gas, grain, and other commodities rushed to increase ruble stocks. By March 30, the ruble was back up to pre-invasion levels (Perry 2022). By increasing the holding of rubles and decreasing USD, the United States overleveraged its position and system, beginning renewed state challenges to American dominance.

The financial struggle between Russia and the United States over Ukraine is not the beginning of the war over the international monetary system. There has long been competition between the United States and China over a currency (Ng 2022). China devalues its currency to make its exports cheaper (McDonald 2015; Navarro and Roach 2012; Scott, Jorgensen, and Hall 2013). However, to directly challenge the United States, China, like Russia, must begin demanding states to hold more renminbi so that trade and exchange might be conducted using the currency. Saudi Arabia is considering the receipt of the renminbi as payment for China's oil purchases (Said and Kalin 2022). If China continues to demand to pay in renminbi (and accepts renminbi as payment), we could see further inflation. This is a challenge to the USD and a new development given the example of Saudi Arabia, a state that exports 25 percent of its oil to China.

Since China emphasizes bilateral trade networks through its One Belt, One Road initiative, it has the latent power to demand indebted and dependent states to be coerced into behaving in the best interests of China (Kim 2019). Coercion may include buying, holding, and using the renminbi as part of China's grand strategy. By leveraging the One Belt, One Road's bilateral makeup, China can pressure weaker states into selling sovereignty for the sake of its power. The more states that opt to trade in renminbi, the more it will add to China's global power and influence. Also, the more states that hold renminbi add to the network externalities of using the renminbi. More countries are using the renminbi now than ever before. In 2016, SWIFT reported that over one hundred countries use China's currency to pay/receive payments in renminbi. Some of these states are undoubtedly small economies. Some examples include Bolivia, Colombia, Mozambique, Namibia, Kuwait, and Georgia. These are relatively small economies but among the largest in Spain (SWIFT 2016). These signals change, and it is an angle that is not discussed.

The idea of network externalities dictates that the more states begin to accept and hold renminbi, the conditions for increasing their renminbi holdings will also grow. States may start selling USD to buy more renminbi. Suppose China continues demanding trade in renminbi, especially using the leverage it acquired over years of creating trade dependencies. In that case, the potential for the renminbi to undercut the USD is real. China's economic power has been positioning itself to supplant the United States. Dollar hegemony could end because of the number of alternatives that could become available. When you consider decentralized cryptos (and soon the centralized cryptos), you might see further destruction of the USD value. In the current inflationary environment, the more USD is sold, the more it will depreciate against the renminbi. The renminbi might soon become a competitor to the United States or a significant disruptor. The renminbi thus presents a clear and present danger to the USD as the world's reserve currency despite its capital controls, not as a potential replacement but as a disruptor.

The renminbi, the ruble, and even cryptocurrencies present significant challenges to the USD. Competitor states such as Russia and China seek ways to circumvent American financial power and control by pushing back. The weaponization of the USD has backfired on the United States. The weaponization of the USD has led to challenges from the renminbi and cryptocurrencies that ultimately threaten US hegemony. There are alternatives to SWIFT; there are alternatives to the USD: the counter-hegemonic challenge of China. At a minimum, these alternatives are serious, and this potential for disruption threatens American dominance (specifically the USD's dominance), especially in the current inflationary environment. This may be part of China's grand economic strategy: an alternative to Bretton Woods institutions through the One Belt, One Road initiative and its international banks, such as the New Development Bank. Due to these challenges, the United States may soon be unable to control the world's financial system. Using economic power, the United States risks further eroding its power, mainly if punishments result in punishment.

Please note that we now see increased state competition levels, regardless of levels of integration, interdependence, the strength of regimes and institutions, the power of norms, and notions of expected behavior. The issue here is that states pursue state interests in terms of power regardless of globalization. The struggle is not simply for security but for control of the international system itself. Indeed, globalization was itself a product of the US power. Now that the United States is in decline and other authorities are rising, state competition has returned. A significant part of this competition seems to be over financial power. The United States has dominated the financial system since the end of World War II. By overleveraging its position, the United States has pushed rogue/pariah states, such as Russia and Iran, to circumvent sanctions by any means necessary. China and Iran barter, avoiding American sanctions, while Russia forces dependent states to trade in rubles. China's One Belt, One Road is another way to facilitate its rise. China now has the potential to coerce states into trading in renminbi. Looking at the potential destabilization, the United States is now on the back foot. The following section will elaborate further on the challenges posed by China and Russia as they position themselves for multipolarity.

In retrospect, it all seems so apparent due to the focus on the state, state power, and the perspectives of non-hegemonic states (states other than the United States at the time). Sometimes, former great powers seek to return to their former greatness. But more often than not, states seek security. Greatness is a guarantor of security, as Mearsheimer (2001) would argue. This is not to say that powers always succeed in their search for greatness, but it does mean that states primarily seek security. In particular, Russia's geopolitical position is marked by a physical landscape that encourages attack. It is true that in the past two hundred years, Russia has been invaded from the west three times through the lowlands of Eastern Europe. This might explain Russian revisionism in light of NATO expansion (Sharafutdinova 2020).

China is also seeking to regain its former glory since the "Century of Humiliation" (Wang 2020; Hussaini 2020; Mayer 2018). Western powers and Japan are the main inhibitors of its growth and domination. Overturning such humiliation through acts of prestige would mean overturning the status quo, such as its separation from Taiwan. This might bring further instability to the international if the United States and other states feel threatened by this action. The issue is that Russia and China both see it in their interests to modify the old order through the power to gain power. Annexing Taiwan and Ukraine is a way for China and Russia to do this. It is in the interests of the United States to prevent this because it desires to protect its status quo or the old order. Any new order will ultimately threaten the United States. Hence, we now have a conflict of interest.

The study of political interests is at the backbone of international politics. Institutions and ideas also matter, but interests (and power) are not to be ignored. A succinct definition follows: interests are anything that makes a state more secure (Nuechterlein 1976). Security is defined by the ability to remain autonomous and sovereign, an independent unit operating within the international system (Waltz 2010). If the Soviet Union placed nuclear missiles in Cuba, it would be in the interest of the United States to get them out. Hosting missiles in Cuba would result in moments of blackmail for the United States, severely limiting its foreign policy choices. If the United States is dependent on other states for oil, it would be in its interests to manage supply chains and the oil price. Again, the oil price holds the United States hostage by limiting the number of foreign policy choices available.

In another example, if any state is planning on attacking the United States, or inflicting economic damage upon it, then it is in the interest of the United States to act to neutralize the source of that vulnerability.

Currently, the United States is defending against a multiplicity of interests. It is balancing against Russia, China, and Iran, providing counter-terrorism support to African, Middle Eastern, and Latin American states, funding NATO while some members free-ride, and giving aid to developing conditions (US Build Act), all the while trying to improve the lives of over 325 million citizens. The United States also contributes to the bulk of the funding for major international institutions like the World Bank, the World Health Organization, and the International Monetary Fund. The end of the Cold War brought on this imperial overstretch, making the American decline almost inevitable (Kennedy 1988). Why has the United States taken on this much responsibility when founded on principles of non-intervention? All this can be boiled down to a straightforward argument: the wealthier the state, the more it needs to expand outward to secure its interests in terms of wealth through power (Zakaria 1998). A state must therefore expand to survive in a zero-sum world. Hence, throughout its process of economic expansion, the United States had to increase its presence overseas, thereby creating international interest. These interests need defending to sustain development and prosperity at home. The point of no return regarding isolationism came in 1945 with the end of World War II. From the American perspective, the Soviet Union and its expansionary ambition had to be stopped. This author believes that the United States was threatened by the power of the Soviet Union, not by its economic system. Power is the ability of one state to make other states behave in a way that benefits the interests of the former (Morgenthau 1985). The United States (and the Soviet Union) wanted to avoid being dominated. Regardless, the Cold War was over in 1991.

As stated, the American unipolar moment resulted in Russia and China's designs on the system. The 1990s was a period of great humiliation for Russia. During this time, specifically in 1996, Russia, under President Boris Yeltsin, chose Yevgenii Primakov to assist in developing a coherent foreign policy strategy. The resulting Primacov Doctrine hoped to reestablish Russian greatness. Russian power would mean a relative reduction in American power, bringing the world back into bipolarity (as we will see, multipolarity). The Primacov Doctrine focuses on five major points:

1 Russia is an indispensable actor in global politics, pursuing an independent foreign policy.
2 Russia's foreign policy is surmised within a broad vision of a multipolar world managed by a group of nations.
3 Acceptance of Russia's primacy in the post-Soviet space and Eurasia is fundamental to all diplomatic overtures to the nation.
4 Russia is fundamentally opposed to any expansion of NATO.
5 Partnership with China forms a cornerstone of Russia's foreign policy (Kanikara 2019).

To simplify, Russia hoped to regain its lost position and prestige by reducing the relative power of the United States. This was primarily done to achieve a better international defensive strategic position. It would require coordinating with China, increasing China's power, and ultimately bringing the world into a new multipolar balance. This process is to remake the international political structure: it is security politics by other means. The reason is simple: Russia did not feel secure after losing the Cold War to the United States. Russia, therefore, desired to erode United States' power, not just absolutely but relatively, by working together with China. Hence, the formula is simple: American overextension plus the balancing efforts of Russia and China brought the end of the unipolar era; power shifted from the status quo to revisionist forces resulting in the current world order. This need for China and Russia to overturn the system did not spontaneously occur; it was decades in the making.

The world of the 1990s is long gone; our world is more similar to the pre-World War I era, a sort of high-tech, more globalized Concert of Europe; at least, that should be the aim. Even as they compete, great powers must mark out areas sacred to their security. Without this demarcation, great powers may crash into one another leading to war. In this day and age, the era of nuclear weapons, states must pay extra care to avoid war and escalating a conflict. The United States, given the hegemonic proclivity toward expansionism, unknowingly helped the multipolar process along. In retrospect, it seems clear that declarations of the end of history were inherently premature. If the structure of the international system, anarchy does not change, then state behaviors remain the same. Even though the United States dominated the global system after the Cold War, any chance of perpetual unipolarity was simply short-sighted and incorrect.

To conclude this section, Kenneth Waltz once remarked: "Balances disturbed will one day be restored" (quoted in Ikenberry 2002, 4). This means that eventually, American unipolarity would be eroded and replaced by either a bipolar or multipolar system. The latter seems true today, especially in light of the discussions given in the previous section. China and Russia are challenging the United States on many fronts, not just economic. China and Russia are threatening to overturn the status quo, pushing their security agenda at the expense of other states. Russia is in the middle of invading Ukraine, while China is threatening to annex Taiwan and all of the South China Sea by exerting its military power in those areas. Even though the United States remains the dominant military power, Russia and China are rising to challenge their position. The explanation is simple: the United States wasted its influence in Afghanistan and Iraq, and Russia and China rose quickly. The structure of the international system has changed, and all three actors must adapt to change to avoid direct conflict.

There have been other changes in the world. Domestically, ideology has been evolving. *The End of History* hypothesis has proved fragile even with its expectation of democracy being victorious. The United States, the bastion of democracy, is currently facing a crisis. Donald Trump's right-wing populism and reactions to it are now challenging the internal regime security of the country. Many countries are also experiencing this pivot to the right: Brazil, France, the United Kingdom, Hungary, and Poland, among others, are all on the political right, and many not within that spectrum see it as a threat to the country. Russia and China's authoritarianism is also seen as an attractive model. Democracy is clearly under threat.

Ideology Continues: An Essay on Domestic Politics

International politics is governed by a two-level game, not just the systemic level (Putnam 1988). The masses may overturn the world order if the right circumstances exist. Globalization, and the idea of global cosmopolitanism, was revolutionary. A rising tide was supposed to raise all boats, but it has not happened. The election of Donald Trump and the rise of right-wing populism are now the antitheses of the thesis of global cosmopolitanism. And no one ever predicted or thought Trump would win or that right-wing populism would be a possibility.

Significant changes are happening in domestic politics that Friedman, Fukuyama, and others simply could not fathom in the 1990s.

The election of Donald Trump came as a surprise to many. To people living in swing states like Pennsylvania, Michigan, Ohio, and Wisconsin, it was a bold opportunity to put someone in that spoke to their need to bring back jobs, avoid foreign wars and entanglements, and bring wealth back into their hands. The message was like that of Bernie Sanders, although his message was drowned out by his self-immolation; calling yourself a socialist in any form will not win you the popular vote or even a primary. Of course, Hillary Clinton made sure of that. So, Donald Trump's message won where it counted. The message here is clear: the structure of the international system may change due to leadership changes. This neoclassical realist argument explains that intervening variables transform state behavior within anarchy (Rose 1998). The leader chooses the path forward and the foreign policies that are necessary to survive any threats and challenges to survival.

Politics is an elitist game; the poor have little time to organize and strategize, which is part of the problem. Trump played an intelligent game by reaching out to the working class and promising that he would bring back jobs. Trump presents himself as a president representing two types of people:

1 Disenfranchised by contemporary capitalist practices
2 Those who wish to avoid foreign entanglements

These policy recommendations are essential in a multipolar world. However, Trump's quick fixes are interesting and may seem unrealistic and dangerous to the functioning of the US economy. Tariffs may encourage other states to do the same, leading to reduced market access. The manufacturing and coal industries have been brutalized due to free trade. Trump promises to bring those jobs back through protectionist measures like tariffs. China has responded in kind. China holds significant American debt and dollars and has been selling these on the open market, depreciating the US Dollar.

Furthermore, the US government must ensure that the economy works for everyone. Economic instability will only encourage people to move toward authoritarianism. The government thus has not filled its purpose, that is, to protect people from sometimes destructive forces of the economy. The state must be able to compensate the losers of globalization, which has yet to be addressed. A free market economy changes rapidly, and sometimes, people are left behind. Adam Smith would advocate free education that would retrain those people disenfranchised by the system. We must take all of Smith's lessons to heart, not just the ones we like, or capitalism cannot work. Writing in April 2019, 102 years after the first major revolution in Russia, we have learned much. First, revolutions appeal under poverty and strife conditions (Kassab 2016). Second, wheels are never successful. There has never been a successful revolution because the initial promises were never kept. Utopian principles are harder to make a reality than it is to convey in words. All wheels resulted in the institution of tyranny after people were used to overturning the reigning government. The twenty-first century seems to be a time of revolutionary nostalgia but with little desire to overturn the system. The reason is simple: democracy and capitalism won (Fukuyama 1992). This may be correct in that these two political structures are the future of politics.

Beginning our discussion, the ideal of democracy emerged with the American and French revolutions in the early eighteenth century. Democracy gave people the hope that their interests could be represented in government. In the American case, developing a constitution helped protect individual rights and freedoms against a tyrannical government. The French Revolution was far less successful, leading to tyranny and bloodshed, culminating in Emperor Napoleon Bonaparte. Yet, the ideas of democracy spread all over Europe. This was because the status quo, what one may term conservativism, as a political ideology, served the few at the expense of the masses. The failure of the French Revolution and its conservative counterrevolution helped solidify this belief (Ozinga 1991, 11). One participant in the process, Francois-Noel Babeuf, felt that the revolution and its violence did not go far enough to usher in a utopia (James 2011, 81). He argued that all property must be owned in the commune for true equality. The effects of the Industrial Revolution further established this perspective. This was a terrible time for society. The sudden increase in economic inequality, environmental destruction, and societal change brought their desires for democratic change closer to Babeuf than Thomas Jefferson.

Under these conditions came the term "communism" in 1840 (Pipes 2001, v). To recall, the French and American revolutions brought forth the ideas of equality and freedom. Half a century later, these ideals

were seemingly left to rot. People, even children, worked in difficult and filthy conditions (Jennings 1936, 422). Communism hoped
to answer the problems of the working poor, and people began to
organize to better themselves (Smelser 1959, 341). Karl Marx understood that world history is based on class struggle (Marx 1967, 90).
Instead of the liberal ideas of freedom and equality, the conservative
status quo dominated (Hobson 2004, 246). Marx and other communists
understood that the state itself was the problem and hoped to overturn it in revolution. Taking hold of the state would control production
and create a new era (Marx 1967, 90). Attempts were made in the
revolutions of 1848 to accomplish this goal. Revolutionary attempts
were made throughout Europe's major cities (Priestland 2009, 33–34).
However, they fizzled out as workers' movements were too weak to
face the state (ibid 36). Conservative parties in Europe responded with
reforms to placate and satisfy the working class. Barrington Moore
argues:

> One striking fact about the course of conservative modernization
> is the appearance of a galaxy of distinguished political leaders:
> Cavour in Italy; in Germany, Stein, Hardenburg, and Bismarck,
> the most famous of them all; in Japan, the statesmen of the Meiji
> era ... All were conservatives in the political spectrum of their
> time and country, devoted to the monarch, willing and able to use
> it as an instrument of reform, modernization, and national unifica-
> tion ... one may even detect a contribution of the ancient agrarian
> *regimes* to the construction of a new society ... In taming the labor
> force, it again played an important role, by no means entirely
> repressive.
>
> (Moore 1993, 440)

Otto von Bismarck was a significant figure in the effort to placate the
working class. Consolidating Prussian and then German state power,
he initiated a top-down reform of German political society to ensure
political stability. Bismarck launched a revolution from above to provide security for the ruling classes. He introduced several reforms for
internal security purposes, borrowing directly from socialist ideas.
Policies such as a social safety net for the unemployed, social insur-
ance for the sick and elderly, and compensation for work-related
accidents, among other reforms, helped immensely (Steinmetz 1993,
5). The reforms were inherently transformism, the Gramscian concept

that describes the hijacking of radical ideas (the taming of the labor force mentioned above) by the ruling class to modify them to guarantee the longevity of current hegemonic ideas and thus ruling class dominance (Quataert 1993, 163). Bismarck called these policies to state socialism and destroyed the communist movement until after World War I.

The popularity of communists and socialists stemmed from the economic depressions of the 1870s and 1896. Other than that, socialists and communists are usually shunned in society during vibrant economic times. There were many socialist parties in Europe before World War I; the most organized was the German Social Democrats, which had 850,000 members. Many other nations had stronger social democratic parties, such as Finland and Sweden. France's party wasn't that large, but no mass parties were ever popular in France at that time. The growing popularity of the German Social Democrats led to the establishment of the Centre Party of Germany, a Catholic Centrist party that was all-encompassing. This curbed the increasing strength of the German Social Democrats.

Further, within socialist parties, thousands of interpretations and cults of personalities are trying to vie for power. Within these divisions are the seeds of destruction for socialism and other extreme ideologies. Most people prefer a stable existence. This makes *transformismos* a powerful force in politics resulting in the dominance of center politics like social democracy.

Social democracy is the synthesis of the conservative thesis and the communist antithesis. Conservatism and communism are untenable, but when they conflict, they create a better political system for political and economic stability. Combined with a balance of power foreign policy, the second part of the nineteenth century up to World War I was far more successful than if the status quo prevailed.

The twentieth century has seen a significant political change from the so-called Bolshevik revolution to the Iranian revolution. Indeed, the twentieth-century revolutionary governments are being overturned in favor of something more globally status quo: socialist governments in favor of capitalism, nationalist/Islamic style governments pushing for democracy. The twenty-first century seems to be a time of revolutionary nostalgia but with little desire to overturn the system. The reason is simple: democracy and capitalism won; Francis Fukuyama (1992) may be correct in that these two political structures are the future of politics.

This has not happened, especially in the United States. The political left in the United States runs from the left but governs from the right. The two-party system pushes the extremes into the center; today, it seems this center is more right than left. As a result, the United States may have gotten more conservative because of the power that owes money in politics. A two-party system is far easier to bribe.

Inequality has increased over the decades because of policies that suit the rich (Stiglitz 2012). This is interesting but more relevant to the book because of the relationship between economic inequality and the two-party system. As a result, it is efficient for businesses to work with only two political parties.

Ultimately, the Democrat Party has moved to the right. Issues like race relations, women's rights, and LBGTQ rights are all heart of the democratic platform. However, these are only to gain the consent of those who see themselves as liberal. The economic policies are the same. The power of dark money in elections serves the financial interests of those paying, not the working class. These policies are inherently more conservative than the Progressive strategies of middle-out economics. Success in the Democratic Party must be on par with the success of major corporations. Further, groups and issues we consider "marginalized" are now being taken in by significant corporations. In a piece written by Chinyere Ezie for the Washington Post:

> As the mountains of rainbow shirts, shorts, and shimmery trimmings have piled up, the message to LGBTQ communities this and every June of late is clear: We want to help you celebrate your identities—and we want you to return the favor by buying our products … But a critical contradiction attends brands' marketing of Pride apparel. The global garment industry is defined by exploitative labor conditions that render workers—particularly queer workers—vulnerable to abuse. For all the alleged solidarity brands telegraph to their queer consumers, it is rarely extended to queer workers in the factories where apparel is sewn.
>
> (Ezie 2019)

Capitalism penetrates identity making it the same. This establishes consent surrendered by marginalized groups, those most hurt by the system. Another example would be *Resistance Ice Cream* by Pecan Ben and Jerry's:

Together, Pecan Resist!
Alongside all those nutty chunks, this pint packs a powerful message under its lid: together, we can build a more just and equitable tomorrow. We can peacefully resist the Trump administration's regressive and discriminatory policies and build a future that values inclusivity, equality, and justice for people of color, women, the LGBTQ community, refugees, and immigrants. Pecan Resist supports four organizations working on the front lines of peaceful resistance, building a world that supports their values.

(benjerry.com, accessed July 10, 2019)

Capitalism, the act of buying a tub of ice cream, is an act that builds resistance. By equating opposition to capitalism, what is one left with fundamentally? Such practices can be found all over the world. Furthermore, what is more surprising is the reaction to Trump's ban on the LGBTQ community from serving in the military. Why would anyone want to fight for a country that has worked against their interests for so long? One cannot generalize entire communities of people. Still, it is hard to imagine people clambering to be a part of the culture of war, especially in a state that is pushing back on their rights and freedoms. All of this is quite absurd. If we assume that capitalism exploits and alienates the most vulnerable in society, these marketing campaigns entrench American cultural hegemony.

Elites and the working classes seem to cooperate, ending the class struggle. Symbols and issues of capitalist resistance (and resistance against Trump) are being appropriated to achieve unity between elites and those protesting for electoral victory and further enshrine free market capitalism into society. Resistance figures push for the symbolic assimilation of anti-capitalist figures like Che Guevara while at the same time (maybe indirectly) supporting widening economic inequality. Coupled with this, there also seems to be an excellent disdain for actual impoverished individuals who vote conservatively from time to time (Michigan, W. Virginia, Ohio, and such). The Democrats used to be the party of the working class, but somehow, that has been forgotten in favor of major corporations. Capitalism may stay as it is now part of individual identities. The same can be said about democracy, as we have come to accept anything democratic as inherently good, further enshrining this end of history.

The new world order envisioned by liberals discusses the pressures of global market forces on the nation-state. Foreign direct investment and businesses moving production plants and manufacturing infrastructure to low-wage states put pressure on home states to lower wages to remain competitive. This hallowing-out pressure is remarkable and has left much of the working class in developing states without jobs. It is easy to recommend retraining, but that leaves aside the human component: is the person willing and able to pick up and move? This disembedded understanding of the labor markets is precisely what Polanyi predicted in his article "The Great Transformation." In the social sciences, we divorce unnecessary variables to create an elegant theory with explanatory power; a theory explains one aspect of our world. These endeavors usually neglect the emotional, spiritual, and other components that make us human. This leaves us little power to predict human behavior in the long run. However, there has been a significant populist backlash. Many in Britain and the European Union, like the United States, feel disenfranchised by the political system. The British, like Trump supporters, are not stupid. They have real problems and want to be heard. Their frustrations are simply improperly channeled. Angry people do not think; they just do. The elite must be made to understand this as the masses, as always, wield serious power. The Brexit vote is a case in point: people voted to leave to teach the government a lesson because it felt good to send a strong message. Hence, the most interesting thing about Trump is his supporters, who are not stupid but in a difficult socio-economic position and see them as an inconvenience; nothing more than the America of yesterday will soon be replaced. Their political voice must be heard. The Brexit vote is a case in point: people voted to leave to teach the government a lesson because it felt good to send a strong message.

The future of the international system will, in part, be determined by the citizens of the United States. Given that and the function of Putnam's two-level game, there are four Americas split under four ideological perspectives:

1 Trumpian or Americanism: country-first, protection of economic interests remain untested in this age of globalization. Will globalization be reversed, and what will happen to relationships between states? He sounds like an authoritarian type of populist, which is relatively new for the United States. Supporters like him because he's the kind of leader who would break the rules and make this country more affluent. He may violate the rights and freedoms of others, like Muslims and Mexicans, but not "ours." This is fair

game for people feeling cheated or disenfranchised by the political system.

2 Social Democratic: Sanders and Warren are not socialists, but they are those with significant views that the United States has issues that need government intervention. The Green Party may use their work as a social democratic vehicle like Norway. This is a major dividing factor in the Democratic Party.

3 Clinton, elites: a continuation of Obama's principles. Clinton's agenda is internationally interventionist and the maintenance of the neoliberal economic status quo.

4 Regular GOP: status quo American conservative, neoconservative foreign policy, neoliberal economic policies, and conservative social views.

The ideas of these competing ideological groups will not simply go away; major organizing factors for these groups are merely buzzwords and symbols.

What does the future hold for US domestic policy? First, democracy will remain strong. Trump does possess a strong character with authoritarian characteristics. He admires strong leaders, but that does not mean eradicating democracy and the evolution into a fascist state. The US government comprises three independent branches of government. The independent legislature, the bicameral Congress composed of the House of Representatives and Senate, is still independent; Democrats even lead the House. There is also an independent judiciary branch that strikes down unconstitutional acts of the president. If anything, the Trump presidency has woken the people and members of government, reminding them that democracy is something that takes work; it does not happen automatically. Checks and balances remain, and democracy in the United States remains robust and secure.

Donald Trump's presidency looked remarkably similar to past presidents. Building a wall has been a path to border security since President Clinton's era. President Obama was referred to as "Deporter in Chief" by journalist Jorge Ramos. Ramous argued directly with Obama, saying, "If you, as you're saying, always had the legal authority to stop deportations, then why did you deport 2 million people?" (Ramos quoted Steinbuch 2014). Donald Trump has decided to keep Guantanamo Bay open, an institution opened to support terrorists in limbo after 9/11. On the economic side, the Obama administration has already placed significant steel tariffs on Chinese steel, but who knows what will happen if other, more damaging tariffs are set on China.

In sum, the domestic source of global change must be considered as the world moves toward multipolarity. The instability of globalization is a significant source of domestic instability, giving cause to the domestic environment. Such change is also felt globally and may be connected to the broader dialectic.

Conclusions

We are entering a multipolar world order. The United States must share the stage with China and Russia. This requires all states to prioritize their state goals carefully. The United States must maintain a specific sphere of influence to ensure security. The same goes for Russia and China. These states aim to maintain a balance of power. This world is thus very much different from the world imagined in the 1990s by Fukuyama and Huntington. Capitalism is also very other from the traditional Marxist understanding. Corporations have taken up the anti-capitalist cause, which ultimately undermines it.

References

Bergsten, C. F., and Green, R. A. (2016). *International Monetary Cooperation: Lessons from the Plaza Accord after Thirty Years.* Peterson Institute for International Economics and Rice University's Baker Institute for Public Policy, Houston.

Bordo, M. D. (2020). The Imbalances of the Bretton Woods System 1965 to 1973: U.S. Inflation, the Elephant in the Room. *Open Economies Review, 31*(1), 195–211.

Bothwell, L. E., Greene, J. A., Podolsky, S. H., and Jones, D. S. (2016). Assessing the Gold Standard—Lessons from the History of RCTs. *The New England Journal of Medicine, 374*(22), 2175–2181.

Boughton, J. (2001). Northwest of Suez: The 1956 Crisis and the IMF. *IMF Staff Papers, 48*(3), 425–446.

Cesarano, F. (2006). *Monetary Theory and Bretton Woods: The Construction of an International Monetary Order,* Cambridge University Press, New York.

D'Emilio, F. and Moulson, G. (2022). "Kremlin demand rubles for gas, EU leaders push back," *Associated Press,* March 31.

Ezie, C. (2019). "PRIDE FOR SALE" *New York Times,* June 20, 2019. www.washingtonpost.com/graphics/2019/opinions/pride-for-sale/#Rainbow%20Police.

Fukuyama, F. (1992). *The End of History and the Last Man.* Free Press, New York.

Gilpin, R. (2001). *Global Political Economy: Understanding the International Economic Order,* Princeton University Press, Princeton.

Higgins, M. and Klitgaard, T. (2007). "Financial Globalization and the U.S. Current Account Deficit" *Federal Reserve Bank of New York in Economics and Finance,* Federal Reserve, New York.

Hobson, J. (2004). *The Eastern Origins of Western Civilization.* Cambridge University Press, Cambridge.

Holm, M. (2017). *The Marshall Plan: A New Deal for Europe.* Taylor and Francis, Florence.

Hussaini, H. (2020). The Historical Sources of Nationalism in Contemporary China. *Technium Social Sciences Journal, 13*(1).

Ikenberry, G, J. (2002). *America Unrivaled: The Future of the Balance of Power,* Cornell University Press, Cornell.

Jennings, W. W. (1936). *A History of Economic and Social Progress of European Peoples.* The Kernel Press, Lexington.

Kainikara, S. (2019). Russia's Return to the World Stage: The Primakov Doctrine – Analysis. *Eurasian Review,* November 5, 2019. www.eurasiareview.com/05112019-russias-return-to-the-world-stage-the-primakov-doctrine-analysis.

Kassab, H. S. (2016). *The Power of Emotion in Politics, Philosophy and Ideology,* Palgrave, New York.

Kennedy, P. M. (1988). *The Rise and Fall of the Great Powers: Economic Change and Military Conflict from 1500 to 2000,* 1st ed. Random House, New York.

Keohane, Robert, O. (1984). *After Hegemony: Cooperation and Discord in the World Political Economy.* Princeton University Press, Princeton.

Kim, S. C. (2019). China and Its Neighbors: Asymmetrical Economies and Vulnerability to Coercion. *Issues and Studies – Institute of International Relations, 55*(4), 1–25.

Krasner, S. D. (1983). *International Regimes,* Cornell University Press, Ithaca.

Marx, K. (1967). Manifesto of the Communist Party. In C. Cohen (Ed.) *Communism, Fascism, and Democracy: The Theoretical Foundations,* University of Michigan, New York.

Mayer, M. (2018). China's Historical Statecraft and the Return of History. *International Affairs (London), 94*(6), 1217–1235.

McDonald, J. (2015). "China is taking steps to devalue its currency; global exporters could take a hit due to cheaper yuan". *Capital, Annapolis, Md.*

Mearsheimer, J. J. (2001). *The Tragedy of Great Power Politics,* Norton, New York.

Moore, B. (1993). *Social Origins of Dictatorship and Democracy.* Beacon Press, Boston.

Morgenthau, H. (1985). *Politics among Nations: The Struggle for Power and Peace,* 6th ed, McGraw-Hill, New York.

Navarro, P. and Roach, S. S. (2012). China's Currency Manipulation: A Policy Debate. *World Affairs (Washington), 175*(3), 27–37.

Ng, D. (2022). *Currency Wars with China and Japan in Western News Magazines.* Taylor and Francis, New York.

Nuechterlein, D. E. (1976). National Interests and Foreign Policy: A Conceptual Framework for Analysis and Decision-Making. *British Journal of International Studies, 2*(3), 246–266.

Oatley, T. (2010). *International Political Economy,* Pearson, New York.

Ozinga, J. (1991). *Communism: The Story of the Idea and Its Implementation,* Prentice Hall, Englewood Cliffs.

Perry, J. (2022). "USD/RUB back to pre-invasion levels; watch USD/PLN and USD/HUF" *City Index,* March 30 www.cityindex.co.uk/market-analy sis/usdrub-back-to-preinvasion-levels-watch-usdpln-and-usdhuf/.

Pipes, R. (2001). *Communism: A History,* Modern Library Edition, New York.

Priestland, D. (2009). *The Red Flag: A History of Communism,* Grove Press, New York.

Putnam, R. (1988). Diplomacy and Domestic Politics: The Logic of Two-Level Games. *International Organization, 42*(3), 427–460.

Quataert, J. H. (1993). Women's Work and the Early Welfare State in Germany: Legislators, Bureaucrats and Clients before the First World War. In S. Koven and S. Michel (Eds.), *Mothers of a New World: Maternalist Politics and the Origins of the Welfare State* (pp. 159–187). Routledge, New York.

Quiggin, J. (2004). The Unsustainability of U.S. Trade Deficits. *The Economists' Voice, 1*(3) https://doi.org/10.2202/1553-3832.1020.

Rose, G. (1998). Neoclassical Realism and Theories of Foreign Policy. *World Politics, 51*(1), 144–172.

Said, S. and Kalin, S. (2022). Saudi Arabia Considers Accepting Yuan Instead of Dollars for Chinese Oil Sales. *Wall Street Journal,* March 15 www.wsj.com/articles/saudi-arabia-considers-accepting-yuan-instead-of-dollars-for-chinese-oil-sales-11647351541.

Scott, R., Jorgensen, H., and Hall, D. 2013. "Reducing U.S. Deficit Will Generate a Manufacturing-Based Recovery for the United States and Ohio. Ending Currency Manipulation by China and Others Is the Place to Start", Economic Policy Institute Report, Ohio.

Sharafutdinova, G. (2020). *The Red Mirror: Putin's Leadership and Russia's Insecure Identity.* Oxford University Press, Oxford.

Smelser, N. (1959). *Social Change in the Industrial Revolution: An Application of Theory to the British Cotton Industry,* Routledge, New York.

Steinbuch, Y. (2014). Obama Bristles at "Deporter-in-chief" Label in Fusion Interview *NY Post,* December 10, 2014. https://nypost.com/2014/12/10/obama-bristles-at-deporter-in-chief-label-in-fusion-interview/

Steinmetz, G. (1993). *Regulating the Social: The Welfare State and Local Politics in Imperial Germany*. Princeton University Press, Princeton.

Stiglitz, J. E. (2012). *The Price of Inequality: How Today's Divided Society Endangers Our Future* (1st ed.). W.W. Norton & Co, New York.

Strange, S. (1988). *States and Markets,* Pinter, London.

SWIFT. (2016). "More than 100 countries are now using the RMB for payments with China and Hong Kong." *SWIFT.com,* October 27 www.swift.com/news-events/press-releases/more-100-countries-are-now-using-rmb-payments-china-and-hong-kong.

U.S. Department of the Treasury. (2022). Press Release: U.S. Departments of Treasury and Justice Launch Multilateral Russian Oligarch Task Force. March 16, 2022, https://home.treasury.gov/news/press-releases/jy0659.

Viksnins, G. J. (1973). Dollar Overhang and Development Assistance. *Inter Economics, 8*(3), 78–80.

Waltz, K. (2010). *Theory of International Politics,* Addison-Wesley, Reading, MA.

Wang, Y. (2020). 'The Backward Will Be Beaten': Historical Lesson, Security, and Nationalism in China. *The Journal of Contemporary China, 29*(126), 887–900.

Zakaria, F. (1998). *From Wealth to Power: The Unusual Origins of America's World Role*, Princeton University Press, Princeton.

5 Exploring the Unknown Future

Introduction: Nationalism to Globalization: Yet the State Remains

Chapter 2 onward summarized the previous two hundred years: the international system shifted from multipolarity in the nineteenth century to bipolarity for much of the twentieth century. There was a short period of unipolarity until 2008 when many have now acknowledged multipolarity. Through these transformations, there were experiments in mercantilism and free trade globalization. Many, like Fukuyama and Friedman, thought it impossible to return to a nationalist, power-centric, and multipolar setting. In contrast, others saw a return to state conflict and increased imperialism (see Chapter 3). Chapter 4 critiques the *End of History* hypothesis, showing that the progress imagined was collapsing. Rather than linear history, it has been dialectical or possibly cyclical (it is too early to tell). In other words, is history a product of clashing ideas (the dialectic), or is it an observable process of repeating patterns of behavior (cyclical)? This is a difficult question to answer without engaging in historicism. Historicism is an effort to shape the future by reading the past. It is not a discussion of history but a foretelling of the future (von Mises 1985, 211). To recall, Politicist analysis deconstructs any ideological dedication, including historicism when appropriate, and tests the fortune tellers with the benefit of hindsight.

Avoiding the Politicist tendencies of our international political predecessors (discussed in Chapter 3) is essential to isolate trends and explain future ramifications. This chapter will describe six possibilities, given the existing developments that shape international politics. The first two discuss whether states will continue to disintegrate. Will

DOI: 10.4324/9781003468677-5

more breakaway regions within existing states win independence, or will there be an attempt by existing states to consolidate? Newly independent states like South Sudan, East Timor, and Kosovo are often weak. These are threatened as many exist alongside power-seeking states that may seek to recapture the lost territory. Given the need for security, will states put aside their differences to form more significant, more powerful states? The European Union might serve as a prime example. The second two illustrate trends of continued state competition within anarchy. The essential argument here is a Waltzian (2010) one: security will continue to dominate international politics unless the anarchical structure of the international system itself changes. What trends point to the global government in light of Covid-19, climate change, and financial instability? The final two prospects discuss the possibility of competing imperialism and neo-medievalism. The term new empire and great power competition over weak states produce complex behaviors based on exploitation resulting in competing loyalties. This creates a challenging political environment. This chapter explores these six possible futures for global politics without selecting a possibility.

State Integration or State Disintegration: Past and Future Trends

As of July 2022, there are 193 independent states in the international system. Over time, this number will either increase or decrease. Some nations like Palestine, Catalonia, and Kurds are seeking independence. There are also regions seeking to break away from an existing state, such as Bermuda (UK), West and western Libya, Donetsk People's Republic (Ukraine), Bougainville (Papua New Guinea), and so on, that may also seek independence. The United Kingdom itself may devolve into the Kingdom of England and Wales if the Scottish manage to secede. Russia, China, and India are vast multi-ethnic, multi-lingual societies. The United States might also break up, given the vast divide between liberals and conservatives, especially in Texas and California. This presents an interesting problem for the international system. The more states in the global system, the more complicated it becomes for scholars to explain and predict the balance of power and the vast array of foreign policy options available to states.

On the other hand, as more states secede, there is an increase in the potential for conflicts, such as the long-lasting conflict between

Ethiopia and Eritrea (Steves 2003). Further, the smaller the state, the less wealthy and less powerful (or weaker) that state becomes (Kassab 2015; 2018; 2020). The smaller the states become, the more they exist. The more states in the international system, the more likely great powers will seek to absorb them through force or economic domination. Does this mean that smaller states will eventually reunite to consolidate resources, manpower, and military might to fend off challenges from larger states? Will state capabilities evolve similarly to modern Germany's, going from the Holy Roman Empire to the Confederation of German states and then the German Empire?

The center of this analysis is not simply the anarchical nature of the international system but the nature of state power. While nations may seek independence from an oppressive "other," such independence may only be the beginning of difficulties. States still function to survive by providing security and economic well-being to citizens (Mearsheimer 2001). States may employ several strategies to defend against a much larger state. For instance, several small states may unite, pooling their resources to balance against a much larger state (Walt 2005, 113). The European Union is an apparent attempt to pool resources. After the fall of the Soviet Union, many eastern European states saw their future tied to NATO and western European powers. The result was not simply to join NATO but to bind economies and political destinies into one major superstate similar to that of the United States. While states like Czechoslovakia broke in two, and the states of the former Yugoslavia sought independence, in the end, separate states united again within a much larger bloc.

People form nations, and those nations seek self-rule within an independent state (Hobsbawm 1990, 6). Hobsbawm explains that there are objective and subjective definitions of nation and nationalism. Objectively, he uses the example of the Tamil-speaking people of Sri Lanka. The Tamil-speaking people speak a different language from the majority of persons in Sri Lanka who speak Singalese. This fact forms the basis of Tamil nationalism and the effort to win independence (ibid). However, there are also subjective explanations in that if persons understood themselves as different from the more significant state, then these individuals may come together to form a nation (ibid). Hobsbawm states that "if enough inhabitants of the Isle of Wight wanted to be a Wightian nation, there would be one" (ibid). This effort requires a genuine effort by individuals to develop consciousness of individuals to the "imagined community" formulated

(Anderson 1983). This is referred to as "nation-building" as persons have to actively work toward developing a separate cultural or linguistic identity to justify the political separation. Many scholars consider nationalism an ideology that impacts international relations (Coakley 2012; Ozkirimli 2010). For this reason, the international system went from just a handful of European states before the Napoleonic era to 193 states today. The French Revolution was the birthplace of nation-building, as linguistic qualities united the French-speaking people under a single banner of so-called "brotherhood." Such a development significantly impacted subsequent nationalist movements in Germany, Italy, Greece, and other Balkan states culminating in several international crises, such as the Moroccan and Balkan crises before World War I. Indeed, the nineteenth century saw the rise of nationalist movements that continue to shape Europe's politics even today. These ideas have extended to the developing world and helped usher in nationalist movements. While Edward Said is correct to say that the post-colonial world is ultimately a different entity than that of Europe, it is clear that elites in the developing world borrowed from European ideas of nationalism, capitalism, and the welfare state, all part, and parcel of the nation and state-building endeavors. These Euro-centric now form the basis of non-western states' function. Said differently, the state system and nationalism, regardless of their western origin, fundamentally shape the politics of individuals globally.

While one can argue that Euro-centric notions of states and nationalism affect the growth and development in places like Africa, the Middle East, and Latin America, it is significant to note that such problems were initially present in the early days of European statehood. Arjun Chowdhury (2018) argues that most states are weak and fragile, with the stark inability to deliver public goods and security to the vast majority of their population. He argues that this weakness is not a deviation from the norm but the norm (bid 1). Indeed, this was certainly the case in the nineteenth century when European states like Italy may not have provided such security (bid 4). Today, the United States is finding it difficult to provide affordable health care, housing, and even safety (crime in major cities); it becomes clear that the state is failing to carry out its ultimate function: providing security. The less secure a state becomes, the more vulnerable it is to attacks from other states.

While states present the greatest threat to other states, it is also important to note the growing number of non-state threats operating freely in the international system. Terrorists and organized criminal networks are now more powerful than states. Mexico and most of the conditions of Central America cannot neutralize their organized criminal groups that, on many occasions, engage in terrorist-style violence. Afghanistan is now a hub for terrorist groups and can freely produce and trade opium. As these problems persist and get worse, states will become increasingly insecure.

In the face of state and non-state threats, weak states have little choice but to rely on great powers to solve their problems (Kassab 2015). However, if the United States (for instance) is unwilling or unable, it falls to them to help themselves. Coordinating responsibilities and pooling resources may be needed to remain secure. This requires complex diplomatic negotiation but also deep cooperation. Walt, in "Alliance Formation and the Balance of World Power" (1985), discusses the factors states use to evaluate threats: the strength of the threat, its geographic proximity, its offensive capabilities, and its intentions. The closer a more powerful, aggressive state is to other relatively weaker states, the more vulnerable states will be driven together. Walt refers to this as the balance of threat theory. Intentions, not power, will enhance responding alliance structures. This said, if the global system shifts to a multipolar world order and truly becomes self-help without excellent power support, weaker states would certainly respond through their robust alliance systems.

Moreover, since threats are not simply other states but also internal issues, it is safe to assume that a deeper, more intricate relationship is needed. The benefits derived from integration will become significant. Similar to the history of the European Union is the use of functionalism. The state, on its own, cannot solve global problems or be self-sufficient. By opening up to trade and cooperation, states can reap enormous benefits. The spillover effect from increasing interdependence means that gradually, a coal and steel trade area can become a free trade and eventually a currency and political union. Hence, the states of Europe, even the smallest ones, can wield enormous clout by banding together. As one of the founders of the European Union, Jean Monnet remarked: "People only accept change when they are faced with necessity, and only recognize necessity when a crisis is upon them" (quoted in Cross 2017, 1). Hence, for weak states to balance against much larger threats and neutralize violent non-state challenges, it might be seen as necessary for nationalistic states to put aside their differences and form political unions. As nations within states seek independence, the difficulties of remaining solitary, secure, and self-reliant in the face of much larger, more powerful threats (state and non-state alike) may bring those nations together again.

This section thus presents an obvious choice for weak states seeking security: either internally balanced or externally balanced. External balancing or alliances are a fruitful choice. However, transnational threats of the magnitude we see today present an even more significant threat to national and human security. Conversely, a nation may seek an independent state to enhance self-rule for psychological or self-esteem needs. However, the challenge of survival and ruling within a self-help system becomes obvious since independence is achieved. States may seek to bind together to protect interests in the face of more powerful threats. Indeed, there are examples of this in the past. There were failed projects in the latter part of the twentieth century, like the United Arab Republic between Egypt and Syria from 1958 to 1961 and then the Federation of Arab Republics between Egypt, Syria, and Libya from 1972 to 1977 (Jankowski 2001). These unions collapsed soon after formation due to leadership and policy squabbles. Leadership disagreements and internal conflicts also caused the West Indian Federation to collapse after two years, from 1958 to 1962 (Lewis 1999). These two specific cases generally see political instability and fragility coupled with significant economic under-development. Member states of these unions now face global and domestic problems on their own, with each state employing resources toward a state bureaucracy. Those resources may best be used toward development. By burden-sharing, these states may be better able to neutralize threats.

Conversely, there are unions in the world that are blossoming. The European Union is one example. Member states have gone through a long period of integration, with national security becoming a significant part of their raison d'etre. Specifically, France and Germany hoped to avoid war with each other by integrating their economies. With this, these states sought to put their differences aside, specifically their conflicting territorial claims, and look forward to a much brighter, peaceful future. This led to increased prosperity and further integration, giving spillover benefits.

On the other hand, member states face different threats to their existence which may inhibit cooperation. States may shirk their responsibilities altogether and free-ride by leaning on other states. For instance, European Union states are also members of NATO. Many member states have evaded their military duties by relying on the United States. This, therefore, might encourage resentment and be a source of conflict and disunity. This might be likely due to different threats. For instance, Poland and other eastern European states may consider Russia the most significant threat to Europe. Other states like the Netherlands might consider climate change to be most pressing due to the lowland nature of their territory. Spain and Portugal may consider undocumented migration and terrorism the most significant threat due to their proximity to Africa, specifically the failed state of Libya.

The broader successes of the European Union and the difficulties surviving the tumultuous international system may play into what Kenneth Waltz called state socialization (Waltz 2010, 127–128). States study the behavior of others and will emulate successful foreign policies and eliminate failed policies. So, if states perceive the European Union as an altogether successful union (more successful than failure), we may begin to see similar geographic unions worldwide. Indeed, the East African Federation and the Visegrád Group are budding examples of this. Of course, it may be too early to present such an argument, but it is essential to watch these developments closely.

The problem for states is that the international structure continues to exist. States must protect themselves and their interests from other states and non-state actors. This has proven difficult, especially given the experiences and challenges of Covid-19. However, this competitive state system will persist unless states decide to create a one-world government.

Global Government or the Statist Status Quo?

The international system is changing from unipolarity to multipolarity (Kassab 2020; 2023). This systemic change is creating changes in state behavior toward competition for power, economically for resources, and militarily weak states. This competition makes cooperation more difficult, especially between the international system's significant powers and those caught in between. One may argue that global mutual problems may increase the likelihood of states working together, but this has yet to be seen. Climate change and the Covid-19 outbreak remain pressing global issues, and states have not put aside their differences to address these threats to human existence. The

Covid-19 outbreak was particularly shocking. Rather than sharing resources, China hoarded masks and other PPE supplies necessary to fight the pandemic (Togoh 2020). In May 2020, the Department of Homeland Security (DHS) reported that China hid the pandemic's seriousness while cutting domestic mask production and increasing mask imports, thereby creating a shortage (Weissert 2020). Instead of communicating that the outbreak spread quickly throughout China, the Communist Party of China (CCP) allowed the disease to propagate globally. So, from the DHS report, rather than cooperating, China may have used the pandemic to inflict severe pain throughout the international system (Togoh 2020; Weissert 2020). This is not to say that Covid-19 was purposefully developed or released but that China did nothing to slow the spread. Instead, China failed to notify states of the World Health Organization (WHO) of the possibility that a deadly disease was quickly spreading. This lack of communication and transparency points to the essential competitive international system where cooperation is difficult to achieve.

While the international system has severe transborder issues that cannot be neutralized by one state alone, states have not come together to counteract them adequately. Terrorism, organized crime, environmental degradation, climate change, economic instability like financial crises, and health issues are all sources of global destabilization requiring state cooperation. International regimes and institutions often become part of state struggles, making them useless in the face of real problems (Keohane 2012). It is easy to say that cooperation will solve these problems. Still, state behaviors are driven by mistrust, making collaboration difficult, if not impossible, as relative gains are given priority over absolute profits resulting in suboptimal outcomes (Grieco 1988). Waltz (2010) argues that these behaviors cannot change unless the structure of the international system changes. The design of anarchy promotes states' self-help security behavior producing internal balancing (military buildup) and external balancing due to an overall lack of an overarching orderer. This structure fosters mistrust and competition and creates war as states seek survival. This means that irrespective of globalization and the gains from free trade, states may still go to war due to the international structure. Waltz's argument remains significant because the global political structure he described remains the same.

Excellent power conflict is still possible unless the international system changes from anarchical to hierarchical. This may happen in two ways. First, a state might be able to amass considerable power to defeat every state and create a world empire. Mackinder (1904; 1942) discusses this. Mackinder discusses the significance of the Eurasian heartland or pivot area in these two works. The specific of this area is left vague and imprecise (Mackinder 1942, 597) but somehow includes some or all parts of Ukraine, Russia, Belarus, Georgia, Iran, Azerbaijan, Central Asian states, Mongolia, and the Arctic islands (Mackinder 1904, 312). This area is significant to world security because of its resources, both natural and human, as well as its terrain, making it hard to attack and easy to defend. Russia controls much of this space but remains divided (see the previous state list). Dominating the heartland will allow for supremacy of the entire Eurasian space, what Mackinder calls the World-Island. Controlling this area has its advantages made even more significant with access to warm water ports allowing for the isolation of other continents like the Americas (outer islands). Mackinder thus argues:

Who rules East Europe commands the Heartland;
Who rules the Heartland commands the World-Island;
Who leads the World-Island commands the World (Mackinder 1942, 50).

Thus, whoever can effectively control Eurasia might be able to control the world. Conversely, Mearsheimer (2001) has argued that the stopping power of water (high seas and oceans) makes world domination an expensive and almost impossible endeavor. However, Mackinder argues that holding or organizing specific geopolitical areas may help achieve that goal (Mackinder 1942). If power can amass a strong, numerically superior navy, then it may be able to close off the world's maritime checkpoints, including:

- The Malaccan Strait in the Indian Ocean
- The Gulf of Hormuz in the Middle East
- The Suez Canal linking the Mediterranean and the Red Sea
- Panama Canal linking the Atlantic with the Pacific Ocean
- The Strait of Bosporus (Turkish Strait) linking the Mediterranean Sea to the Black Sea
- The three Danish Straits linking the Baltic Sea with the North Sea
- The Strait of Bab el-Mandeb forms a gateway for vessels to pass through the Suez Canal on the east coast of Africa (Maritime Insight News Network, March 6, 2021).

China already boasts the largest navy in the world by the number of ships (Burgess 2020). It may be able to overwhelm the international system by capturing and defending every single major chokepoint, halting world trade in one fell swoop. Such an act would enable China to take over the world. Hence, if China overpowers Russia or manages to control its economy (made possible by western isolation after the Ukrainian war), it will be able to essentially control the heartland and, thus, the world with its numerically superior navy. Technological advancement now makes it possible to control the world; shooting down satellites using hypersonic missiles will destroy both communications and international visibility. Overwhelming cyberattacks will effectively shut down the internet, making it difficult for governments and citizens to conduct business. The way artificial intelligence is developing should concern any international relations and military science expert. The world is changing quickly, and technology is making the world smaller, almost making physical space insignificant. While the Russian war shows that supply chain management is significant (Stackpole 2022), there are now developing rockets that hope to send supplies to the frontline of battle almost immediately (Szondy 2021). The question becomes whether technological innovation will reward or incentivize offense similar to World War I, where railroads and trains offered benefits to the state who mobilized first.

The above is not to speculate but to argue that it might indeed be possible for powers like China or the United States to change the international structure from anarchy to hierarchy, given their power position within the global system. Given China's revisionist tendencies since the reign of Xi Jinping, conquering the world would make China the political center of a world empire. The United States, in fear of losing its international system, might very well operate in the same manner (Gilpin 1988). The global system might also be hierarchical if states willingly surrender their sovereignty to an international body. What is the potential for this to happen?

Trends in international and domestic politics do not point to the willful surrender of state sovereignty in favor of world government. For instance, nationalism is still a relevant force. The BREXIT vote pointed toward retaining British power in the face of regional pressure to remain. There are also those states in the European Union like Hungary, the Czech Republic, Slovakia, and Poland (Visegrad Four [V4]) that firmly advocate for sovereignty, locking out migrants from entering their state in apparent defiance of European Union rules (Rettmann 2022). While there is pressure from human rights groups to let migrants freely move between states, states are not giving in; the need to protect the rule of law and the status quo remains a significant factor for governments. The same can be said in the United States. Donald Trump was elected in 2020 partly because he promised to build a border wall between the United States and the southern border with Mexico. As a Republican, he gained support from conservatives. He received criticism from the Democratic Party. The border wall was deemed a racist institution that must be abolished. The election of Joe Biden brought hope for a return to normalcy that the border wall would essentially be torn down. However, it was reported by White House Press Secretary Karine Jean-Pierre that the United States would be "plugging in gaps" in dangerous areas that migrants cross (Schwab 2022). Casillas (2022) reports that sanctuary cities, where undocumented migrants can be protected and work without fear of deportation, face increased pressure from the thousands bussed in from border states.

Increased financial pressure and cities like Washington DC or local budgets are brought upon. Thus, it would seem that economic pressures are building on local governments. These governments prioritize local and domestic politics rather than actively working toward the free movement of people like Las Americas Immigrant Advocacy Center, RAICES, Texas Civil Rights Project, The Florence Immigrant, Refugee Rights Project, and so on (see more at nnirr.org, accessed August 4, 2022). These humanitarian non-state actors are seeking to improve the lives of undocumented migrants, seeking

> the enfranchisement of all immigrant and refugee communities in the United States through organizing and advocating for their full labor, environmental, civil, and human rights. We further recognize the unprecedented change in global political and economic structures, which has exacerbated regional, national, and international migration patterns. We also emphasize the need to build international support and cooperation to strengthen the rights, welfare, and safety of migrants and refugees.
>
> (bid)

Essentially, the aim is to destroy the state through the free movement of people across borders, including the right to vote. While these groups are still subordinate to the state and the law, they are formulating a policy that could destroy borders soon.

Other aspects of global governance that point toward the structure of the international system remain anarchical rather than hierarchical. Existing international bodies, like the United Nations (UN), WHO, and International Monetary Fund (IMF), are still represented and led by states. The P-5 (United States, United Kingdom, France, China, and Russia) veto power remains a central feature of the United Nations Security Council. These states will veto any matter that conflicts with their national security interests. However, other institutions that have little to do with politics become political. Their mission statements reflect that institutions like the WHO aim to promote global health. However, state interests still find their way into governing politics. During the Covid-19 pandemic in 2020, China refused to allow Taiwan into the WHO even though Taiwan's infection rate remained low (Chen and Cohen 2020). During the beginning of the outbreak, the WHO was accused of towing China's line about the impossibility of human-to-human transmission. During the same time, Taiwan was developing systems to track the virus and slow its spread (bid). Further, when asked why Taiwan was not allowed to join the WHO, WHO senior advisor Bruce Aylward hung up, refusing to discuss the matter further (bid).

Another issue with international institutions is that many are now directly competing. Bretton Woods institution banks like the World Bank and the IMF are challenged by China's financial institutions like the New Development Bank and the Asian Infrastructure Investment Bank (Rana 2019). Instead of working through already established banks, China prefers to create its own bank, forwarding its particular agenda. Essentially, international institutions that are supposed to bring states together to solve problems and promote economic development, health, and overall prosperity are subject to state competition.

The state system seems to remain from the trends presented in this and the previous section. The abstraction presented by Kenneth Waltz describes the political reality. States, militaries, and interests are the primary mover of international political outcomes. However, specific facts on the ground cannot be ignored. Great powers like the United States, China, and Russia oppose regional imperial powers seeking to expand their geopolitical and economic spheres of control. In many instances, loyalties cross and go beyond the nation, embracing economic and political spheres that complicate the study of international politics.

Competing Neoempires and Neo-medievalism[1]

This section explores new potential governance ideas by proposing a theoretical framework examining the interaction of weak states and great power grand strategy within an international system of anarchy. Grand strategies are the overall survival strategies of states. All states have grand strategies as all states seek or function to survive as independent political units (Balzacq and Reich 2019). The survival threats to great powers and weak states are fundamentally different. Great powers pursue prestige against other great powers seeking the same (Taliaferro 2006, 40). This means undermining the other's power, position, and reputation in a zero-sum world. On the other hand, weaker states suffer from systemic vulnerabilities, given their stark underdevelopment. Weak states trade their political power with great power for aid or other economic assistance. This locks weak states into dependency and underdevelopment. If enough weak states support a particular great power, that great power will become more powerful and prestigious relative to competitors. This forms world systems' dependency networks based on trading political support for aid, creating a political unit that goes beyond the state. I term this new empire. Creating dependency networks described by the World-systems Approach creates competition for weak state loyalties that defy balance of power expectations.

To explain these state survival behaviors reflected by new empire and neo-medievalism, we must synthesize Structural Realism and a World-systems Approach (to understand the role of weak states). When great powers buy weak states, we see the formulation of economic dependencies, and core-periphery subjugation, for excellent power prestige. Given underdevelopment, great powers take advantage of the weaker state's need to survive. World-systems Approach holds excellent explanatory power in this regard. If great powers trade aid for power, weak states become part of a new international sub-structure. I conceptualize this sub-structure neoempire. Unlike a state, a new empire is a collection of states that unify under one great power. Unlike empires of old, weak states can still exercise some autonomy, precisely overlapping core-periphery world-systems relationships with others competing for great powers. There is still some flexibility to engage other great powers, unlike bandwagoning. I call this behavior playing the field. Competition continues in this regard.[2] Weak states benefit from this parasitic behavior but become dependent in the process, never entirely escaping weakness and underdevelopment.

Neoempire denotes domination by underscoring political/military elements and overall psychopathic/exploitative behavior. Competing world dependency systems form the Structural Realist international system due to the wealth and power gained from exploiting weaker states. Studying great powers as states is outdated. The existing competitive international system (independent variable) contains dependency networks (intervening variable) constructed by great powers to explain prestige-seeking behavior (dependent variable).

The competition between new empires might be a continuation of international politics, given the presence of many weak states with competing allegiances. Hegemony usually leads to overextension as beneficiaries seek to alter the rules to further their power. Structural Realism is used to understand the role of power, and World-systems Approach to understanding the route to power may be the correct course of action for this time. Weak states have proved vital to great powers. What else explains the constant interventionist policy by the United States, the Soviet Union, and China in the past? The United States, through the Monroe Doctrine, made it a point to protect its sphere of interest, the states of Latin America, from the grasp of other powers. The Soviet Union used much weaker states of Eastern Europe as a buffer and intervened in Afghanistan. The Afghanistan adventure helped bring down the empire. After the failed American war in Vietnam, China also tried a failed intervention in Vietnam. The United Nation's Responsibility to Protect (R2P) exists because more extraordinary powers are interested in safeguarding liberal global political structures and mechanisms. Additionally, several international regimes and institutions led by the United States since 1945 have existed solely to float a global economy by assisting weak states in their development agenda. China and other nations of the BRICS (Brazil, Russia, India, and South Africa) are now building their banks and institutions, world systems, to counter the United States' influence regarding developing countries or weak states. Such patterns of behavior fit across the global board. While such involvement is costly, the competitive nature of the anarchical international system forces great powers to engage in these capability-draining activities. If great powers do not, others will fill that void, gaining prestige. Considering the transactions that occur, borrowing from the World-systems Approach, we may be able to understand further the forces that shape the international system's balance of power. The argument then follows: the state as the center of the study of international relations has become increasingly irrelevant over the past seven decades. At one point, it was okay for a state to rely solely on internal mechanisms for economic growth. Once growth hits the ceiling, states must reach outward to ensure continued economic expansion. Anarchy adds another variable: military power and competition. If one great power begins to expand outward, other great powers must follow suit to maintain power symmetry. Economic growth was never low politics. Wealth from economic relations can potentially translate quickly to military power. Here follows the contradiction of the Hegemonic Stability Theory: powers rise within a manufactured system only to overthrow it. Seeking hegemony is like digging one's own grave. This dimension then follows economic expansion which then forces other states seeking survival to expand. This was the reason for the war discussed by Vladimir Lenin. Economic relations between great powers and weaker units of the world system result in power acquisition for great powers. Hence, weak states are systemically crucial to great strengths to increase wealth and, thus, power and control.

This combinational approach offers a description of grand strategy today, given the interaction of great powers and weak states and their diverse motivations of prestige and survival. Their interaction forms an international system given various grand strategies. Great powers want to survive as great powers and seek to be treated as great powers. Prestige is a "...state's reputation for having power, especially military power- and status- that is, a state's recognized position within the international hierarchy ..." (Taliaferro 2006, 40). This is not a rational determination but a cognitive, psychoanalytical, and irrational one. These prestige-seeking units have international interests that eventually undercut other great powers leading to balancing behavior and eventual (or potential) conflict because, in the minds of these great powers, they deserve it more than others do. This explains why great powers act as psychopaths, killing, exploiting, and interfering in the affairs of weak powers. Their behavior makes little sense except at the systemic level as a part of the systemic practice. Prestige-seeking behavior, in standard Structural Realist language, is zero-sum; it means that great powers compete for prestige.

On the other end of the power spectrum, weak states are systemically vulnerable states in need of aid and resources to survive the fluctuations of the international system (Kassab 2015). Weak states are vulnerable to sudden economic, political, environmental, and health disasters. They also lack the resilience to deal with such shock due to a lack of capability. As a result, the prospect of long-term survival is inherently questionable. Lack of resources necessitates behavior that defies usual bandwagoning and can only be thought of within a new standard of conduct I call "playing the field" (bid). Playing the field means weak states engage in parasitic behavior with great powers in conflict to extract as much benefit, such as aid and preferential trade agreements, as possible. This will assist in their survival needs as independent political units. As a result:

Great powers seek security through the balance of power both internally and externally to sustain prestige.

Great powers seek out weak states to maintain this prestige, especially relative to the attention of great powers. This is traditional great power behavior with an element that considers relations with weaker units.

Due to their inherent systemic vulnerability, weak states seek survival as independent political units. As a result, they seek relationships with great powers on opposing ends of the balance of power.

Using great powers in such a manner does not come without a cost, as certain political favors must be traded. Behind these grand strategies is a network of elites benefitting from exploiting the global poor. When these networks come together, they create a new structure of the international system that goes beyond existing theories. Thus, the balance of power system today differs from before (nineteenth and twentieth centuries) due to the presence of many weak states. Weak states become vital en masse to great powers. Without weak state support, great powers are denied severe influence in the international system, especially within international regimes, organizations, and other forms of global governance. There are some continuities, however. While different in the European and Westphalian sense, weak governance units existed before decolonization. While playing the field is a rational choice for weak states, they lock themselves in the world-systems dependency network (Jacobs and Rossem 2016, 377). This dependency keeps weak states weak or underdeveloped and great powers strong. Great powers need weak states to rely on them, as such reliance is essential to feel like a prestigious, great power, and this is why great powers create these dependency networks. Weaker units must continue selling themselves to great powers to survive, given short-term demands resulting in overlapping loyalties discussed by neo-medievalism. Neo-medievalism sees the international system as structured by "overlapping authorities and crisscrossing loyalties" (Bull 1977, 255). Hence, states are not these unitary actors posited by realism but rather a complicated mess of actors pursuing various and often contradictory interests. For favor, weak states play the hands dealt to them: selling their political autonomy for economic aid. Alone, this is altogether benign. Unified, weak states offer great powers political support and legitimacy at international institutions and other global governance forums. Given their weak status, they present no real threat to any great power alone. Great powers fight for the control and affection of weak states to deny rivals. The international system, then, is not a chessboard. I posit that there is another game at play: Go (Kassab 2015). Go is a Chinese board game in which players seek control of the spaces on the board. The winner is the player controlling most areas on the board. The pieces are weak states; the players are great powers. In essence, neoempires make weak states vulnerable and exposed to exogenous shocks (e.g., economic shock) that perpetuate the need for aid and other forms of help.

Neoempire illustrates the systemic behavior of great powers today. Moving away from the outdated and obsolescent concept of the state, neoempire hopes to explain the behavior of great powers together with weak states as an operative unit. Neoempires are political and economic subsystemic units of governance that operate within an international system. Through world-system dependency networks, great powers encourage cooperation and subordination to accumulate power and wealth to protect global prestige. They function together not simply regionally but are deterritorialized, meaning the units in question transcend time and space in their movement. Neoempires are bound by rules, regulations, expectations, and sociopolitical and economic relations that encourage cohesion through economic transactions and political coordination. Neoempires are similar to empires without the overarching and obvious centralization of power. Empires differ from neoempires in that weaker units are allowed some freedom of movement but are somewhat bound by the policies of the major partner. Today, the United States, Russia, the European Union, and China pursue such relations. The United

States, through politicized free trade agreements, is the writer of these contracts; weaker states are the consumers and followers in the hope of gaining from these relationships, even as they grow increasingly dependent.

The United States and China, specifically, from their behavior, are quintessential neoempires, given their mutually parasitic relationship with weak states. Weak states enter into relationships with neoempires for their economic development to survive the challenges associated with their endemic vulnerability. Great powers within the new empire hope to gain further wealth and power from their world systems to secure themselves against competing great powers of other neoempire sub-systems. The international system then transforms into a rivalry between neoempires, with weaker states shifting their allegiances to world systems at times within issue areas they gain the most advantage while maintaining good relations with former great powers.

Combining the section's two purposes, I suggest that the international system is one of competing neoempires reflecting the World-systems Approach. Competing world systems continue to shape and reshape the global system's balance of power. Great powers are then motivated to accumulate power and wealth to extend further and ultimately protect prestige, even at the expense of humanity. Go is played to accomplish this, even as weak statuses are unreliable and disloyal. The prestige game is exploitative yet expensive but aims for long-term domination. Such a psychotic and destructive system is continually in flux, as competing neoempires must fight for weak state support incessantly. Without fragile states, great powers would lack recognition and global leadership; what good is being a leader when one has no followers?

Here, I offer up new construction of the international system that takes us in the twenty-first century: the coalescence of two grand strategies: prestige-seeking and playing the field. Given the importance of weak states in anarchy to neoempires, we must consider the structure of the international system to be a balancing act between supranational bodies rather than a balance of power between states. The competition for weak states causes this system due to the behavior of all involved components. Weak states increase the relative power and prestige of great powers or neoempires. This is inherently systems constructive behavior and must be considered in any theory of international politics and grand strategy.

The theoretical expectation is that neoempires are emerging, giving way to a new balance of power driven by world-systems dependency. Dependency is designed to maintain dominance over a country or set of countries for two separate yet interrelated material advantages: wealth and power. Great power cannot have power without wealth and cannot have wealth without power. While realists and Marxists tend to isolate which came first, both are incomplete. There is no divide between these two fundamental parts of domination; to say that there is ignores reality and, ultimately, political outcomes: imperialism's original and new sense. Imperialism, at its core, is "... a relationship of a hegemonical state or nation under its control" (Lichthem 1971, 10). Palma relates to this definition:

> ... the essence of imperialism is domination and subordination, and the concrete ways in which the sovereignty of lesser political bodies can be infringed may be manifested in very dissimilar manners as direct and visible as in colonialism, or as complex and diffuse as in a system of international relations of dependency which distorts the economic development of nations.
>
> (Palma 1978, 882)

The matter, of course, is not simply a division between economic and political power but conjoining. For great power, economic domination is for political purposes. Hence, neoempires are led by mechanisms developed by a network of elites ruling across states, great and weak, and legitimized by the consenting masses of great powers seduced by power and economic wealth. Elite interests are the main reason for the constant need to acquire further wealth and power. Economies must continue to expand, or else elites may face political instability.

In summation, the world's future may reach beyond the state due to the complexity of international politics and global change. Neoempire seeks to describe changes in standards and practices set by great powers since 1945 and the decolonization process. This concept attempts to capture or explain the reality behind great power/ weak state relationships of dependency. The conglomeration of great powers and weaker states will generate unequal benefits, which benefit the more significant component of the singular unit. The great power in question will grow faster than other great powers in the system, especially those neglecting weak states. Theoretically, competition for weak states will intensify over time as the gains from weak states become apparent. From this, we can derive a theoretical expectation we are seeing now: the balance of power will shift to great powers sub-systems that have better relations with weaker states even as they are exploited.

Conclusions

Of these six eventualities, it seems complicated to predict which one will take place as these options are rooted in the reality of our international political order. One thing does seem confident: there is a lack of an overarching order which produces security competition between actors. Sticking to simplicity, the future will remain tumultuous. Actors must continue to depend on themselves for security. Avoiding historicism and remaining true to the duty of explaining and understanding the world, scholars must not engage too heavily in normative thought. The concluding chapters discuss this idea further in the term Politicism. Politicism deconstructs arguments and tests them not empirically but whether or not they meet the criteria of being true theories or just products of the scholars' biases.

Notes

1 This section uses segments of the following work: Hanna Samir Kassab, "Grand Strategies of the Weak States and Great Powers," 2018, Palgrave, pages 1–12), reproduced with permission of Palgrave Macmillan. Some alterations and additions are made.
2 Hence the neo for an altered conceptual vision.

References

Anderson, B. (1983). *Imagined Communities: Reflections on the Origins and Spread of Nationalism.* Verso, London.

Balzacq, T., Dombrowski, P. J., and Reich, S. (2019). "Comparing Grand Strategies in the Modern World" In P. Dombrowski, T. Balzacq, and S. Reich (Eds.), *Comparative Grand Strategy: A Framework and Cases* (pp. 1–24), 1st ed. Oxford University Press, Oxford.

Bull, H. (1977). *The Anarchical Society: A Study of Order in World Politics.* Columbia University Press, New York.

Burgess, Richard R. (2020). Pentagon Assessment: China Now Has World's Largest Navy. *Sea Power*, *63*(8), 6.

Casillas, M. (2022). " 'Unsustainable': Resources Running Out for Migrants Bused to DC". *NBC Washington,* July 18 www.nbcwashington.com/news/local/unsustainable-resources-running-out-for-migrants-bused-to-dc/3103956/.

Chen, Y. and Cohen, J. (2020). Why Does the WHO Exclude Taiwan? *Council on Foreign Relations,* April 9 www.cfr.org/in-brief/why-does-who-exclude-taiwan.

Chowdhury, A. and Oxford University Press. (2018; 2017). *The Myth of International Order: Why Weak States Persist and Alternatives to the State Fade Away.* Oxford University Press, Oxford.

Coakley, J. (2012). *Nationalism, Ethnicity and the State.* Sage, Washington, DC.

Cross, M. (2017). A Europe of Crises. In Mai'a K. Davis Cross (Ed.), *The Politics of Crisis in Europe* (pp. 1–21).Cambridge University Press, Cambridge.

Gilpin, R. (1988). The Theory of Hegemonic War. *The Journal of Interdisciplinary History, 18*(4), 591–613.

Grieco, Joseph M. (1988). Anarchy and the Limits of Cooperation: A Realist Critique of the Newest Liberal Institutionalism. *International Organization, 42*(3), 485–507.

Hobsbawm, E. (1990). *Nations and Nationalism since 1780,* Cambridge University Press, Cambridge.

Jacobs, L. and Rossem, R. (2016). The Rising Powers and Globalization: Structural Change to the Global System between 1965 and 2005. *Journal of World-Systems Research, 22*(2), 373–403.

Jankowski, J. P. (2001). *Nasser's Egypt, Arab Nationalism, and the United Arab Republic.* Lynne Rienner Publishers, Boulder, CO.

Kassab, H. S. (2015). *Weak States and International Relations Theory: The Cases of Armenia, St. Kitts and Nevis, Lebanon and Cambodia,* Palgrave Macmillan, New York.

Kassab, H. S. (2018). *Grand Strategies of Weak States and Great Powers,* Palgrave Macmillan, New York.

Kassab, H. S. (2020). *Weak States as Spheres of Great Power Competition,* Routledge, New York.

Kassab, H. S. (2023). *Globalization, Multipolarity and Great Power Competition.* Routledge, New York.

Keohane, R. O. (2012). Twenty Years of Institutional Liberalism. *International Relations (London), 26*(2), 125–138.

Lewis, J. O. (1999). From West Indian Federation to Caribbean Economic Community. *Social and Economic Studies, 48*(4), 3–19.

Lichthem, G. (1971). *Imperialism,* Penguin, Harmondsworth.

Mackinder, H. J. (1904). The Geographical Pivot of History. *The Geographical Journal, 170*(4), 298–321.

Mackinder, H. J. (1942). *Democratic Ideals and Reality*. Washington DC: National Defense University.

Mearsheimer, John J. (2001). *The Tragedy of Great Power Politics*. 1st ed. Norton, New York.

Mises, L. (1985). *Theory and History: An Interpretation of Social and Economic Evolution*, The Ludwin von Mises Institute, Auburn University, Auburn.

Ozkirimli, U. (2010). *Theories of Nationalism: A Critical Introduction*, Springer, New York.

Palma, Gabriel. (1978). Dependency: A Formal Theory of Underdevelopment or a Methodology for the Analysis of Concrete Situations of Underdevelopment? *World Development* 6(7): 881–924.

Rana, R. (2019). Asian Infrastructure Investment Bank, New Development Bank and the Reshaping of Global Economic Order: Unfolding Trends and Perceptions in Sino-Indian Economic Relations. *International Journal of China Studies, 10*(2), 273–290.

Rettmann, A. (2022). "Poland and Hungary go hard on Belarus migrants", *EUObserver,* January 24, https://euobserver.com/world/154165.

Schwab, N. (2022). "We're not finishing the border wall – just cleaning up Trump's mess: Karine Jean-Pierre says Biden is plugging gaps in Arizona to 'save lives' and calls border walls 'ineffective' in stopping migrants", *Daily Mail,* July 29, 2022 www.dailymail.co.uk/news/article-11062947/Karine-Jean-Pierre-denies-admin-finishing-Trumps-border-wall.html.

Stackpole, B. (2022). "Ripple effects from Russia-Ukraine war test global economies", *MIT Sloan School,* June 28 https://mitsloan.mit.edu/ideas-made-to-matter/ripple-effects-russia-ukraine-war-test-global-economies.

Steves, F. (2003). Regime Change and War: Domestic Politics and the Escalation of the Ethiopia—Eritrea Conflict. *Cambridge Review of International Affairs, 16*(1), 119–133.

Szondy, D. (2021). "US Air Force and Space Force look to rockets to transport supplies", *New Atlas,* June 6, https://newatlas.com/military/us-air-space-force-rockets-transport-supplies/.

Taliaferro, J. (2006). Neoclassical Realism: The Psychology of Great Power Intervention. In J. Sterling-Folker (Ed.), *Making Sense of International Relations Theory,* Lynne Rienner Publishers, London.

Togoh, I. (2020). "China Covered up Coronavirus to Hoard Medical Supplies, DHS Report Finds", *Forbes,* May 4 www.forbes.com/sites/isabeltogoh/2020/05/04/china-covered-up-coronavirus-to-hoard-medical-supplies-dhs-report-finds/?sh=5651254a1dba.

Walt, S. M. (1985). Alliance Formation and the Balance of World Power. *International Security, 9*(4), 3–43.

Walt, S. M. (2005). Taming American Power, *Foreign Affairs, 84,* 5 www.foreignaffairs.com/articles/united-states/2005-09-01/taming-american-power.

Waltz, K. (2010). *Theory of International Politics*, Addison-Wesley, Reading, MA.

Weissert, W. (2020). "DHS report: China hid virus' severity to hoard supplies", *AP News Agency,* May 4, https://apnews.com/article/us-news-ap-top-news-international-news-global-trade-virus-outbreak-bf685dcf52125be54e030 834ab7062a8?utm_source=Twitter&utm_campaign=SocialFlow&utm_medium=AP

Conclusions

History continues. Chapter 4 tests the arguments of Chapter 3. The United States is no longer the hegemon. Further, China and Russia were designed to transform the world from unipolarity to multipolarity. This fact does not mean that China and Russia are the forces of evil. These two states simply felt more secure in a world not dominated by the United States. Russia and China had divergent security interests and sought to defend (or regain) them through multipolarity. Now that the United States is no longer the hegemon, these two states can project power. In many instances, this power is used to alter the status quo. Russia is now at war with Ukraine, and China is threatening to invade Taiwan. If Russia is successful, it will alter the status quo, as Ukraine will no longer be an independent state as it was before. The same goes for Taiwan. Both democracies would be forever altered. Liberal democracy and American hegemony are in retreat in these two cases. American influence seems to improve in other states, such as increased collaboration between Israel and Arab states to contain Iran and its nuclear ambition.

When we take in an event, there is an effort by people to try to connect the dots. We try to figure out what "caused" the event by factoring independent variables. Theorizing comes naturally to people looking for answers. When there is no way to find the answer, we come up with explanations to fill in the gaps. Conspiracy theories are attempts to know the truth without access to evidence. The Politicist predictions of the Post-Cold War period were ultimately conspiracy theories but in a more productive sense. This is mainly because scholars and authors preferred seeing the world as they wanted it to rather than taking on some objectivity. Under the guise

DOI: 10.4324/9781003468677-6

of the scientific method, much of the examined literature is laced with their normative approach. Studying the interpretive framework of those writing in the wake of the Soviet Union's collapse helps us better understand that period's policies. Interestingly, those policies were not designed for the short term, not just the future of world order, but the future of being, doing, and relating to one another. The works of Fukuyama, Friedman, Rice, Krauthammer, Hardt, Negri, and Callinicos were ideologically driven, not scholarly driven. That drive led to inaccurate predictions and the neoliberal and neoconservative policies that ended American hegemony in the world and the rise of China and Russia.

Flawed Predictions and the Centrality of State Power

Scholars and thinkers seek new predictions following significant critical junctures in international politics. While there is nothing wrong with figuring out the future, given current trends, it is difficult to say whether or not such trends will continue in the medium to long run. Since conventional wisdom dictates that a week is a long time in politics, why try to figure out the future of the international order? Further, in international politics, it is essential never to ignore power. Power is about control through military, economic, or seductive soft power (Morgenthau 1985; Car 1978; Waltz 2010; Nye 2004). Many scholars in the previous literature summary made that error. They misunderstood the nature of power, specifically its concentration across multinational corporations and financial capital interests. Real power is military power concentrated in the seemingly permanent state. Changes may result regardless of advances in global markets or the power of non-state actors, but state power drives changes in the international system. The "independent variable" here is changes in the distribution of power (the structure of the global system). The "dependent variable" is state behavior, that is, how states adapt to the network. Due to the anarchical nature of the international self-help system, states automatically seek security. Due to the unipolar nature of the global system, threatened states sought to balance against the United States. This led to two power-seeking behaviors or strategies:

1 internal and external balancing
2 a reduction in American power

These two strategies would or strategies would create a multipolar international system, as competitor or revisionist power increases while the status quo power declines. In this way, Russia and China intend to restore equilibrium in the global system. From their perspective, unipolarity is a gross imbalance in the international system, as the United States dominates international politics. Indeed, the Post-Cold War period is defined by American hegemony as it sought to remake the global system in its image (Rice 2000).

From this, one might conclude that state power remains the most significant factor in international relations. Pre-9/11 scholarship that disregarded this aspect is incomplete and awkward. The Structural Realist critique follows that if the structure of anarchy remains unchanged, then it is likely that state security behavior (especially manifested in the security dilemma) will continue. Regardless of the efforts of individuals, international regimes, and global markets, if the international system is anarchical, then security-seeking behavior will remain. If the structure changes from anarchy to hierarchy, especially with the presence of a world government, it might be possible to end state conflict (Waltz 2010). This critique must be confronted before any prediction of the future of global governance. Scholars such as Fukuyama, Friedman, Huntington, and so on based on their work on the role of power, especially power in defending interests, they might have arrived at different conclusions.

If scholars, policymakers, and other writers had other expectations based on power distribution, their conclusions or predictions would have been very different. John Mearsheimer pursued such research and concluded that great power turmoil is possible (2001). Waltz (1999) explained that power and interests were the main drivers of globalization. Gilpin (2001) understood the economic-political dynamic of international political outcomes. Finally, Zakaria (1998) explained that the more economically wealthy a state became, the more global interests it had to protect and the more militarily powerful it would have to evolve. By focusing on power, scholars arrived at entirely different conclusions from many other scholars. One would expect that the United States would carefully utilize this moment to reposition itself and guard its interests defensively and cost-effectively, beneficial to long-term excellent power positioning. This would have been a realist expectation or prediction, which would inevitably turn out wrong. These expectations would be erased on 9/11, replaced by literature on terrorism and the war on terror. In many ways, 9/11 could be considered an anomaly that took away focus on questions of great power politics and turned it toward terrorism. Now that Osama bin Ladin is dead and the Islamic state is gone (the material aspects, not the cognitive, ideological foundations that remain), it is essential to return to Post-Cold War literature and pick up the conversation where we left off. Perceived insecurity generates conflict. Such security behavior may never disappear unless the system changes (Waltz 2010; Mearsheimer 2002; 2001). This is certainly not a new argument, but the fact remains that many scholars disregarded Structural Realist ideas in favor of other agent-specific explanations that ultimately failed. One only has to look at today's international political concerns (China's rise, Russia's resurgence, deglobalization, etc.). Evaluating competing perspectives is a task worth pursuing as we begin to look back at the past thirty years to understand multipolarity.

The structure of the international system is based on self-help meaning that states must secure themselves as no other authority exists to assist if attacked (Waltz 2010). States, especially great powers, tend to balance against one another when threatened. Power is the basis of threat, meaning that states will not feel threatened by a weak state but by powers with equal or greater capacity. When the Cold War ended, Russia was pushed into a period of political uncertainty and plagued by economic instability. Its near-abroad was incorporated into NATO, increasing its vulnerability. This followed a sort of change reaction that we can refer to as the theoretical expectation of Structural Realism:

Unipolarity -> political uncertainty/desire for security -> balancing
   efforts reordering/remaking -> multipolarity

The Politicist scholars who ignored power politics in favor of studying the power and influence of corporations, civilizations, capitalism, and non-state actors missed these developments completely. Instead, they focused their energies on other trends subject or subordinate to the state's authority (Waltz 1999). This book evaluates and synthesizes these thoughts. It can be considered a contemporary political-historiographical study of the writing of histories, specifically the interpretation of its future.

To understand this effort, it is essential to deconstruct the work of one central figure, Samuel Huntington. In the preface to *Clash of Civilizations*, Huntington writes:

This book is not intended to be a work of social science. It is instead meant to be an interpretation of the evolution of global politics after the Cold War. It aspires to present a framework, a paradigm, for viewing global politics that will be meaningful to scholars and useful to policymakers.

(1997, 13)

This book is not a comprehensive view of the pre-9/11 period. It hopes to put its most significant works into context by focusing on future visions. It aspires to illustrate competing frameworks or interpretations of global politics for that period. It evaluates them in a way that hopes to be meaningful to scholars and helpful to policymakers. The adjectives "meaningful" and "useful" are primary, as any work of social science desires to be both. However, in many respects, Huntington's work was not received by many in this light but instead discarded. Many other scholars like Fukuyama had his work rejected as well. Such is the way of academia. However, this book would like to engage and evaluate these and other such results seriously by comparing the authors' vision or interpretation of the future with what happened—holding aside 9/11 and the focus on terror, which dominated much of international relations, especially American foreign policy and what has happened to the international order. This book argues that the great powers of the global system still matter over violent non-state actors and multi-national corporations, actors that remain subordinate to great powers. Great powers matter most; that power is concentrated and centralized in core economic states rather than dispersed and lacking a center. It also argues that competition is not limited to military or security but also through competing international regimes, financial systems, and, most interestingly, over weak states of the global system. This means that the structure of the international system has not simply changed from unipolarity to multipolarity, but specific elements of the system have been incorporated into it. As such, the global system itself has evolved. By distilling past interpretations, we can understand this evolution better.

Keeping Things Simple: Explaining Structural Realism and Systemic Change

To explain the drive of China and Russia to change the structure of the international system from unipolar to multipolar, we must first understand the nature of the international system. This section builds on Structural Realism and the work of Kenneth Waltz and Robert Gilpin. To these Structural Realist theorists, the international system is a political structure that shapes the political behavior of states within it. It is an independent variable that shapes state behavior (dependent variable).

Conceptualizing what is referred to as an international structure reflects on the international system's transformation, taking note of various continuities and discontinuities that shape state behavior and the foreign policy objectives of leaders living in those times. The first task is to outline what is meant by an international system. Hobsbawm himself described the state of the international order through his work. In *Age of Extremes*, he sees the fusion of economics and politics as the primary driver of state behavior and political outcomes (Hobsbawm 1994, 30). Hobson (2005) agrees with this, saying,

> The economic root of imperialism is the desire of strong organized industrial and financial interests to secure and develop at the public expense and by the public force private markets for their surplus goods and their surplus capital. War, militarism, and a "spirited foreign policy are the necessary means to this end."
>
> (106)

As a starting point, this section will discuss Structural Realism as defined by Kenneth Waltz and Robert Gilpin to show the connections between economic power, military and political power, and the process of systemic change. By offering the connections between these forms of power and systemic change, this section hopes to build a firm foundation to apply the historical perspective of Hobsbawm as we trace the development of the international order for the past two hundred years. By underscoring the political-military and economic connection of the international system, this chapter seeks to better understand the nature of the international system throughout history to prepare for future developments.

To understand what an international system is, we must first understand what composes a theory. A theory is a tool used to explain a social phenomenon (Waltz 1997). From a structural perspective (using that term loosely), an idea is a "picture, mentally formed, of a bounded realm or domain of activity" (ibid 913). As a picture of a particular element, theories "lay bare the essential elements in play and indicate necessary relations of cause and interdependency—or suggest where to look for them" (ibid; Waltz 2010, 1–13). Theories are not supposed to be "realistic" but are abstract ways of thinking about the world. Theories are parsimonious and simply used to give life to facts and circumstances (Waltz 1997, 913). There are varying opinions on what theories should be, but Waltz's idea allows the freedom to be creative and graft various theories together, creating an interesting tapestry with explanatory power.

In a field divided by positivists and anti-positivists, Wæver (2009) sees Waltz's representation of theory as influential yet divisive, neither empirical nor interpretivist. Wæver also sees some significant misrepresentations by scholars regarding Waltz's theory. However, if theory, as Waltz says, is a set of statements that explain laws, and these statements help us explain why these laws exist (Waltz 2010, 5), then what are laws? Laws are facts and descriptions of what happened. They can be judged on whether they are genuine and authentic or false and incorrect. Hence, laws can answer *what questions*. What led to World War II? Laws may give us a step-by-step process of what occurred in the lead-up to the war. Theories answer *why questions*. Thus, to connect these two, laws are anything to be explained by the theory. Since this chapter discusses structures and systems, it is essential to begin with Waltz's understanding.

To understand Waltz's *Structural Realism*, it is essential first to distinguish the unit from the structure. Structures cause behavior in the units. As separate entities from units, structures are governing bodies that shape or direct states to act in similar ways regardless of culture, history, or language. Then, structures are independent variables that cause state behavior (Ruggie 1983, 266). Waltz submits that the international structure is anarchical, and this causes security behavior to attain survival. Security behavior then creates the distribution of capabilities, the makeup of the balance of power, and whether the international system is unipolar, bipolar, or multipolar (Waltz 2010, 72; 92–98). State behavior (a competition that sometimes manifests itself in war) cannot change unless the structure changes from one of anarchy to a hierarchy: a world government, for example. Hence, the laws that led to the onset of the Cold War are uncovered. Threats are generated due to the positioning of two great powers within the anarchical structure. Great power competition resulted from the lack of a world government to settle disputes. As a result, great powers must secure themselves and their interests. A historical narrative cannot tell us that.

The best part of Waltz's theory is that it is a simple, bare-bones theory. Those who see the merit of such theorizing can either use his theory as a starting point or create a new one. Building on the theory or changing it slightly produces interesting results (Kassab 2015; 2018). However, Waltz's simplicity does have its drawbacks. First, it can be quite static in that it may fail to explain alterations or changes in the international system. However, it does define power as the primary mechanism for the international structure. Waltz defines power as "size of population and territory, resource endowment, economic capability, military strength, political stability, and competence" (Waltz 2010, 131). Here, Waltz provides a list of factors that might impact a state's power potential. For instance, increasing military strength, accessing significant strategic resources, and economic growth may help boost state power. It can be assumed that changes in these mechanisms may majorly impact a state's ability to influence international outcomes (the behaviors of other states). Some states may also punch above their weight (Israel, Singapore, South Korea), but Waltz refrains from this analysis. So even though Waltz never delves into changes in the international system's structure, it is assumed that changes in power will change the system.

Other scholars seek to understand changes in the distribution of capabilities over time. Robert Gilpin's work steps into that role by highlighting the central importance of a state's economy. He argues:

> ... over time, the power of one subordinate state begins to grow disproportionately; as this development occurs, it conflicts with the hegemonic state. The struggle between these contenders for pre-eminence ... leads to the polarization of the system ... [which then] becomes a zero-sum situation in which one side's gain is by necessity the other side's loss.
>
> (Gilpin 1988, 596)

Change in the international system occurs alongside changes in economic growth rates across states that are essentially zero-sum and competitive. Suppose the hegemonic, status quo power is not growing as fast as a revisionist or challenger. In that case, the international system may likely change from unipolarity to multipolarity. These changes are ultimately a threat to the status quo. Thus, there is a reciprocal relationship between the state and economic power (Gilpin 1975). Further, if a state's economic power increases, then its state power (military and political power) will also grow. This ultimately means that the wealthier a state becomes within an established international system, the more likely that state will challenge that system. Gilpin looks at the dynamic that governed the Thucydides War and shows regularized patterns of behavior in other moments of systemic war that gave rise to a new international system (ibid 592). In previous work, Gilpin highlights the reciprocal relationship between economic power and military/political power:

> On the one hand, politics largely determines the framework of economic activity and channels it in directions intended to serve the interests of dominant groups; the exercise of power in all its forms is a significant determinant of the economic system. On the other hand, the financial process tends to redistribute power and wealth, transforming power relationships among groups. This leads to the political system's transformation, thereby giving rise to a new structure of economic relationships. Thus, the dynamics of international relations in the modern world are primarily a function of the reciprocal interaction between economics and politics.
>
> (Gilpin 1975, 22)

Hobsbawm (1994, 29) notes this reciprocal relationship between economics and politics. He refers to this as a fusion and notes its continuing presence in the nineteenth and twentieth centuries. It is a repeated theme throughout the book. However, Hobsbawm does not delve into the inner workings of this fusion theme but only alludes to it. One might say he lives in a world of laws. As Gilpin has shown, laws alone cannot connect economic growth and political and military power.

Another scholar, Stanley Hoffman, views systems as "... a pattern of relations among the basic units of world politics" (1961, 90). The state that creates the system creates how states behave with each other. Essentially, an international system is one where one central state, sometimes referred to as a hegemonic actor, structures the autonomy and sovereignty of other, weaker actors in the system (Gilpin 1988). The state will still act independently, but the hegemonic actor's policy options are limited and determined. A state is only as free as the structure of the international system that dictates specific acceptable behaviors. If Iraq wants to invade Kuwait, then the United States (the hegemonic actor) can knock it back into place. If Nazi Germany sought to annex states, then the United Kingdom must be able to neutralize these behaviors and protect the sovereignty of states within its system. If it cannot, then it is no longer the hegemon. The idea is that the international system constructs the behavior of lesser powerful states with it. Larger, more powerful states that can effectively challenge the system might be considered revisionist states. This state seeks to overhaul or overthrow the system and is thus a significant threat to the hegemonic state. Looking at international politics and order through a structural lens, we must first understand these motivating factors of systemic creation and recreation by revisionist states.

Many in the past seemed to hail the end of the state system or the decline of the state's overall relevance. They argue that the state system has been replaced by international commerce, global bodies like the United Nations, or norms of behavior. However, this argument is difficult to make unless one explains the central importance of state security-seeking behavior under the structural conditions of anarchy. In many ways, theories are just tools used to explain the world. Anarchy is an assumption that we make to help describe reality. However, in many ways, this assumption can be considered accurate or factual, as there is no higher authority than the state in the international system. Every state has the autonomy to act as it wishes. This also means states will attack other states for several reasons, including being in their national interests (an ambiguous and subjective term). As long as this anarchy structure exists, the international system cannot change. It will produce state competition and security dilemmas that construct international politics.

Given the summary of Structural Realism, it may seem evident that Post-Cold War scholars missed a primary counterargument: that American unipolarity would be short-lived. If anarchy still exists, if self-help mechanisms still drive states, and if states still seek security to survive, then it would be expected that state behaviors will remain competitive as they always have. An international system is simply an analytical tool that seeks to explain international politics as it acts as a vehicle producing state behavior. The problem for Post-Cold War scholars is that they may have placed too much weight on agents as a vehicle for change, ignoring structures altogether.

The structure-agent debate is summarized in Martin Hollis' book *The Philosophy of Science*. Written in 1994, he must have witnessed the Post-Cold War debates. The structure-agent problem tries to isolate how behavior is produced. There are two approaches: a structural approach in which social forces determine individual behavior and an agent approach in which individuals shape those very social structures (ibid 5). There is also the idea that structures/social forces and agents/individuals shape and reshape one another. The structural approach sees individuals as puppets; their behavior is subject to established norms and expected behaviors (ibid 6). This means that states must abide by and respond to structural forces of self-help as determined by anarchy. Agent analysis looks at the individual actor's freedom to shape those structures. States can act according to what they perceive as their best interests. States might be able to change their behavior if other states are willing to do the same. By freely acting, states might be able to completely circumvent the international system through the force of their behavior. If states change their behavior, then theories like Structural Realism and concepts such as deterrence would be made null and avoided, best relegated to an ancient past. Other theories and concepts like neoliberal institutionalism and globalization would be the future. There would be no need for military power. It was declining in importance and was replaced by notions of interdependence (Keohane and Nye 1989). Hence, one possible reason for many predictions after the Cold War could be due to the structure-agent problem: Post-War scholars like Fukuyama, Friedman, Rice, and Krauthammer simply gave too much weight to the agents. Suppose the United States and other like-minded states could act boldly enough, in that case, they might be able to completely change the international system from a competitive one similar to the Cold War bipolar dynamic to one dominated by democratic, capitalist states with an expansionary outlook. Similarly, Hardt and Negri, Callinicos (Marxists), Mearsheimer, and Waltz (realists) all gave too much weight to their specific understanding of structures. The Marxists had a particular conceptualization of capitalism as a structural force that produced state behavior. They understood that the forces of capitalism would be a disciplinary force to those who did not conform; they were correct about that. However, they seem to have missed the likelihood of state competition between status quo powers and rising powers. Military power and state interests still exist, and this continues to have great power war potential. Also, Marxists tend to focus on Western states as major exploiters. However, China has risen to become a significant core state in its exploitation of the global south. Realists are also at fault. Waltz and Mearsheimer gave too much weight to structural forces and little to agent-driven change.

Indeed, the competitive structure still exists. However, states still were driven to behave in terms of their vision of society. This led, fundamentally, to multipolarity. The United States, driven to expand its free trade and democratic vision, made trade agreements with China to socialize them into becoming democracies. The European Union hoped that with increased trade and investment ties with Russia, a relationship of interdependence and peace would rein in Russian territorial ambition. These two policies failed because of international structures. However, Structural Realism fails to account for state attempts to change the international system through agent behavior. In other words, these behaviors go unexplained by Structural Realism. It might be argued that states may, at times, behave illogically, but this cannot be the case as logic, reason, and rationality were imbued into American and European calculations as sanguine as they may have been in retrospect.

The international system falls into the structural category because it is separate from the agents or units that respond to or are impacted by the structure. The structure of the international system produces behavior for states. Those who argue that teams or agents can shape the structure, such as the arguments of Friedman, Fukuyama, Hardt, and Negri, neglect the power of the structure. Since the structure is a product of anarchy, the distribution of capabilities thus shapes the international order. The agents acting within the structure are subject to the balance of power. Individual behavior is thus constrained, fundamentally, by the state system. The state is separate from the structure, but state behavior denies individual action. The state holds a monopoly on the use of power, the determination of market forces, and the norms we believe in.

The state, because of military power (and the concentration of that power and economic resources), remains a seemingly permanent force since the Treaty of Westphalia and arguably has always existed throughout history as old empires were also units of territory with power centralized in military and government. Any change in the international order would require changes in the international structure. Hence, this may produce incorrect expectations, such as the declining relevance of the state and military power. Indeed, military power and national security are still the most relevant parts of international politics.

Ignoring power structures does not mean they will disappear, as those with power will quickly remind them that it is not absent. This could be why states like Russia, China, and the United States seem to be on the brink of warfare. If the structure of the international system does not change, we cannot expect fundamental changes in the international order. We have not arrived at the End of History nor seen economic power decentralized. Instead, we are witnessing a difference in the international system from unipolarity to multipolarity, similar to those that saw the bipolar system altered into unipolarity. This development is all part of changes in the international order. The international order has shifted several times since the Treaty of Westphalia and the establishment of the state system. Specifically, any period of globalization and cooperation was facilitated by a great power or amalgam/regime of great powers. The following section will discuss forms of globalization since the nineteenth century within this specific lens. It will argue that globalization is a product of state power. As a result, states can undo or dismantle globalization if it is in their best interests. World War I and today's period are part of this process, as globalization was/is being destroyed due to state conflict. In these two cases, the domination of one power (Great Britain then, the United States now) led to globalization, giving rise to rising powers (Germany then, Russia and China now). By tracing this historical process, one might make sense of today's world order.

Final Words

In our lives, we often work toward a specific goal. Sometimes, we never quite reach that goal due to unforeseen circumstances and events outside our control. Like in 1990, we yet again find ourselves at a crossroads. This new world is much like an older one, where states carved out areas of the world for their purposes. This is the political structure of our world today. With time, world politics will come together under a world market. Until that time comes, it helps little to fight the tide of state power and politics. Protecting interests will be at the center of international and global political analysis. If the world becomes more power-centric and liberally minded, it is essential to take stock of history. The balance of power remains the central force behind international peace. Essentially then, there has not been much change since the nineteenth century. There remains a global "Concert of Europe" with one significant difference: the power of non-violent non-state actors. Leaders of citizen groups globally can find and connect to be a force for positive change in the world.

Democratic norms and values are still central to many, even those on the political right. Maintaining free speech and capitalism are still liberal democratic values. So ingrained are democracy and freedom that each remains a crucial platform for all political parties in the West. However, just because these norms are intrinsic, it does not mean they will forever exist in the international order. The challenge from Russia and China may roll back democracy in states in Eastern Europe and the Indo-Pacific as states seek security first and liberty second. This is not to say authoritarianism is inevitable, but one might expect an increase in authoritarianism as the multipolar order progresses (Kassab 2022).

Avoiding historicism and Politicism is key: divorcing oneself from any political agenda may help advance knowledge and help formulate better policies. It remains difficult, especially since individuals are still a part of society. Seeing the bigger picture takes skill and courage. Self-awareness is also necessary to maintain a balanced approach. Taking theory seriously is another essential task. The theory is seen as a dead and outdated methodology, something to be laughed at in the era of regressions. However, theory breathes new life into the tedium of statistics. Those who choose to focus on theory are *big-picture* people, and there will always be a place for that.

References

Carr, E. H. (2001). *The Twenty Years Crisis, 1919–1939*, Perennial, New York.

Gilpin, R. (1975). *U.S. Power and the Multinational Corporation: The Political Economy of Foreign Direct Investment*, Basic Books, New York.

Gilpin, R. (1988). The Theory of Hegemonic War. *The Journal of Interdisciplinary History*, *18*(4), 591–613.

Gilpin, R. (2001). *Global Political Economy: Understanding the International Economic Order*, Princeton University Press, Princeton.

Hobsbawm, E. (1994). *Age of Extremes: The Short Twentieth Century 1914–1991*, Abacus, London.

Hobson, J. A. (1938. *Imperialism: A Study*, G. Allen & Unwin ltd, London.

Hoffmann, S. (1961). *International Systems and International Law. The State of War: Essays on Theory and Practice of International Politics*, Praeger, New York.

Hollis, M. (1994). *The Philosophy of Social Science: An Introduction*, Cambridge University Press, Cambridge.

Huntington, S. (1997). *The Clash of Civilizations and the Remaking of the World Order*, Simon and Schuster, London.

Kassab, H. S. (2015). *Weak States and International Relations Theory: The Cases of Armenia, St. Kitts and Nevis, Lebanon and Cambodia*, Palgrave Macmillan, New York.

Kassab, H. S. (2018). *Grand Strategies of Weak States and Great Powers*, Palgrave Macmillan, New York.

Kassab, H. S. (2022). Internal Security: The Encroachment of State Security on Global Liberty in a Multipolar World. *Democracy and Security, 18*(2), 123–146.

Keohane, R and Nye, J., (1989). *Power and Interdependence,* 2nd edition, Harper Collins, New York.

Mearsheimer, J. J. (2001). *The Tragedy of Great Power Politics*, 1st edition, Norton, New York.

Mearsheimer, J. J. (2002). Realism, the Real World, and the Academy. In M. Brecher and F. P. Harvey (Eds.), *Realism and Institutionalism in International Studies* (pp. 23–33). University of Michigan Press.

Morgenthau, H. (1985). *Politics Among Nations: The Struggle for Power and Peace,* 6th ed, McGraw-Hill, New York.

Nye, J. (2004). *Soft Power: The Means to Success in World Politics*. Perseus Books, Cambridge.

Rice, C. (2000). Promoting the National Interest. *Foreign Affairs*, www.foreignaffairs.com/articles/55630/condoleezza-rice/campaign-2000-promoting-the-national-interest.

Ruggie, J. (1983). Continuity and Transformation in World Polity: Toward a Neorealist Synthesis. *World Politics, 35*(2), 261–285.

Waltz, K. (1999). Globalization and Governance. *PS: Political Science & Politics, 32*(4), 693–700.

Wæver, O. (2009). Waltz's Theory of Theory. *International Relations, 23*(2), 201–222.

Waltz, K. (1997). Evaluating Theories. *American Political Science Review, 91*(4), 913–917.

Waltz, K. (2010). *Theory of International Politics*, Addison-Wesley, Reading, MA.

Zakaria, F., (1998). *From Wealth to Power: The Unusual Origins of America's World Role*, Princeton University Press, Princeton.

Index

Mackinder, H. J. 114
markets 37; free 95
Marshal Plan 85
Martin, L. 39
Marxism 11, 12, 34, 35, 46, 49, 77,
  80, 97, 124, 139; postmodernism
  and 58–62
McGrew, G. 39
McWorld Vs. Jihad 49, 53–54
Mearsheimer, J. J. 41–42, 65–66,
  70–71, 90, 131, 139
military power 56, 58, 137
Milley, M. 44
modern international system
  36–45; globalization and 36–38;
  Hegemonic Stability Theory
  and 39–40; increased technologies
  in 38; power of the state and 38,
  39; proxy wars in 43–44; Race to
  the Bottom (RTB) in 39; realism
  and 41–42; rise of China in 33,
  36, 42–43; terrorism and 41,
  44–45
Molotov-Ribbentrop Non-
  aggression Pact 30
monetary economics theory 6
Monnet, J. 110
Montalcini, R. L. 24
Montesquieu 56
Moore, B. 97
Morgenthau, H. 16
Mussolini, B. 30

Napoleonic Wars 25
nation-building 109
Negri, A. 11–12, 38, 49, 80, 139;
  on empire 60–62; power-centric
  analysis by 71
neoconservatism 10, 12, 49, 62–65,
  101
neoempires 118–125
neoliberalism 10, 49, 55–58, 77,
  101, 139
neo-medievalism 118–125
New American Century 59
New Development Bank 42, 117
9/11 attacks 41, 74, 75, 81,
  131–132

Nola, R. 9
Non-System 86–87
North American Treaty
  Organization (NATO) 36, 41, 51,
  52, 66, 75, 91, 111; expansion of
  70–71
North Korea 76
Nye, J. 37

Obama, B. 81, 101–102
Orientalism 52
Ottoman Empire 26–27

Palma, G. 124
Pax Americana 34
Pax Britannica 24, 34
Philosophy of Science, The 6,
  138–139
Polanyi, K. 100
politicism 9–10, 13, 49–50, 80–82,
  142; American dominance and
  54–55; culture wars and 50–55;
  domestic politics and 93–102;
  future trends and 106–107;
  Marxism and postmodernism
  and 58–62; neoconservatism and
  62–65; neoliberalism and 55–58;
  power transition and continued
  relevance of the state in anarchy
  and 82–93; Russia-Ukraine war
  testing the predictions on 67–73;
  Structural Realism and 65–67;
  summarizing four schools of
  thought in 73–78
politicist analysis: defined 8–13;
  and how it works 12–13;
  methodology in 4–8, 12–13;
  theory and theory-building
  defined for 5–8
Popper, K. 2, 8–9, 11, 13, 14
positivist theories 8
post-Cold War era: international
  system in (*See* modern
  international system); politicism
  in (*See* politicism)
postmodernism and Marxism
  58–62
post-positivist theories 8

For Product Safety Concerns and Information please contact our EU
representative GPSR@taylorandfrancis.com
Taylor & Francis Verlag GmbH, Kaufingerstraße 24, 80331 München, Germany